What People are Saying About Kelsey Harris and this Book

"Kelsey was one of the first people to reach out to me in recovery after becoming newly homeless while pregnant. She didn't judge my constant agitation and inability to cope with real life, but took me under her wing and showed me the real meaning of living in sobriety. She showed me the blessings of embracing such a beautiful life. She ended up becoming one of my closest friends, while simultaneously pushing me to my limits and making me work to become what she knew I was capable of being. We've lived thousands of miles apart for years now, and I still look up to her strength and bravery. I still use the life lessons she taught me from day one. Many people gave up on me, but Kelsey never did. Because of her unending support I'm a homeowner, have a successful career, and above all else, I'm a terrific mother to two amazing children. I am forever grateful for her love and guidance in this life."

– Jordan M. clean since 2012

"When I walked through the doors of Celebrate Recovery in 2014, I was broken and afraid. Kelsey's honest vulnerability in sharing the testimony of how she overcame her dark past gave me a spark of hope, and I asked her to be my sponsor. For the next few years, Kelsey gave of her time and energy to mentor me in walking in sobriety and honesty; a gift that I am eternally grateful for. I can remember sitting with Kelsey in her apartment for hours and hours working on my fourth step—taking an intense moral and spiritual inventory of my life in order to make amends to those that I had hurt in the days of my addiction. Kelsey listened and guided with gentle grace and provided me the judgement-free and loving space that I needed to come to terms with where my addiction had taken me. With Kelsey's support and healthy role-modeling, I was able to bring light into those dark places and share my own personal testimony of victory."

"The first time I heard Kelsey's story I was newly clean and terrified of what my new life in recovery would look like. When I heard her story I thought to myself "If this girl with so many things stacked against her and very little support in her corner, can not only stay clean but can also create a pretty rad life for herself, surrounded by people who love her, maybe I can too." Kelsey's story, along with God's grace of course, very well may have changed the trajectory of my life after hearing it so early on in my own journey. Whether you are an addict, a supporter of an addict, or just need a book you can't put down, *Touching Fire* is definitely a must read!"

"*Touching Fire: From the Flames of Addiction to the Beauty of Redemption* by Kelsey J. Harris is a poignant, powerful page-turning memoir about the author's journey through addiction to self-recovery and spiritual awakening. A masterful first book, from the opening two words, "Bang" and "Clink" as the author is jailed for drug trafficking to the final chapter when she writes, "if we've lived to tell the tale, we should tell it", the story is riveting and meaningful. True characters are well-drawn, and the scenes are vivid. Readers are drawn immediately into Harris' jagged world. Fiery and gripping, the story moves along so seamlessly and intensely that it reads like dramatic fiction. The author's journey takes her through jail, skid row, homeless shelters, hospitals, dysfunctional relationships, a mother's grief, hunger, and emotional pain. As a reader, I was right in the scene with her, suffering for her as she slid into addiction and championing her trials and final recovery. Moreover, sections at the end of each chapter entitled "Reflect" reveal the author's insights about her struggle to overcome drug addiction, self-harm, and self-loathing to become the influential speaker and recovery leader she is today. This book is a lifeline for addicts and those living with despair. I highly recommend it."

— Catherine Lenox, Write Contact

"Every once in a while a book comes along that completely impacts your life! This is one of those books. Full of real-world strategies to overcome the many challenges of drug addiction and reclaim one's life. If you or a loved one is struggling with drug addiction, this book allows you to walk a mile (or two) in the shoes of an addict who made it out. Kelsey Harris is completely transparent in her journey back from addiction, incarceration and homelessness to full recovery and societal contribution. She takes us along the path of discovering her life's purpose to serve others in their own recovery. You will experience both tears and joy as you cheer her way back to freedom, family and God."

— Patrick Snow, International Best-Selling Author of
Creating Your Own Destiny

"First, let me say how proud I am of Kelsey Harris and what she has accomplished since I met her in 2011. She was rough when she arrived at our program and we are structured, but she didn't fight the structure, she found that she could change her life and started making choices to do just that. She proved to be an exemplary client and became our first 'permanent resident' as we embarked on building new housing units. Kelsey was the one we asked to step up and do it with us. Five years later, having worked the entire time, staying clean and mentoring many women, by sharing her story and living out her desire for change, she became the woman God created her to be and it was such an honor to witness. We have kept in touch since the day she walked into the program, sharing her dreams and encouraging her to follow the path she began when she walked through our doors. May the goodness she brought into our lives be what others discover when they read her story."

– Theresa Murphy, Program Director of Precious Life Shelter

"Kelsey gives us rare access to the inner world of an addict all while maintaining her individuality—the spiraling thoughts, distorted beliefs, and at times, the terrifying absence of any thought at all. It's not just a story of substance abuse; it's a revealing glimpse into a mind shaped by survival, stimulants, and deep soul wounds. Sometimes the answer to What is she thinking? is simply—nothing. As she writes, "It's hard to tell where the habit stops and you begin." One moment I was walking with Kelsey through the numbness and chaos of a life of addiction and homelessness, and the next, she'd drop a truth so raw and profound I had to pause, set the book down, and just sit with it a while. This book doesn't just tell a story; it invites us to understand, to believe change is possible, and to move us to compassion."

– Teresa Nickell, author of
***The Girl in Your Wallet* and prison volunteer**

Touching Fire

From the Flames of Addiction to the Beauty of Redemption

Kelsey J. Harris

For Brandon

Contents

Introduction
Burned but Breathing

"Look closer and you'll see something extraordinary, mystifying, something real and true. We have never been what we seemed."

~ Zelda Fitzgerald

You have a story—a testimony that begins in childhood and stretches into adulthood. As the story goes on, you cling to the hope that something better is always just around the corner. If you can make it out of the fire you're standing in now, surely better days are ahead. You tell yourself that you'll find happiness when you are skinny enough, smart enough, or if you pick the right life partner or land the perfect career. *Then* you will stop the behaviors that have been holding you back. *Then* you will step out of the flames you're engulfed in, for good this time.

But what if the flames are burning so hot that all your hopes and dreams are going up in smoke with them? What if this habit that you have or this addiction that you try to hide finally wins, and all that you've been looking forward to "just around the next corner," has been lost in the ruins? Or have you already lost everything and the only hope you have left is in finally letting go of that *one thing* that you can't live without? Are you tired of the chase yet?

I know how that exhaustion feels. I know what it's like to give everything away in exchange for that one thing. That one thing that feels like it's saving you but is silently destroying you. The thing that takes and takes and rarely gives anything back anymore, but it's so rooted within you that it's hard to tell where the habit stops and you begin. I know what it's like to touch the fire again and again to see if it's still hot, even when everyone around you is telling you that you'll be burned. I know the feeling of a life being so interwoven with addiction that I couldn't tell anymore who I was without my drug. We were one and the same.

For years, I imagined what this book might become. I've written and rewritten the story in my mind countless times. In the end, I believe it became what it was always meant to be.

I could have given you endless stories about how bad it really was, filled it with gory details about a life where I was drowning in pain and anarchy, criminal behaviors and chaos. I could have given you details about watching my friends die, participating in drug and gun trafficking, becoming a thief and a liar, and losing my identity and self-worth to the streets. If you're holding this book, chances are you already know what that life looks like—either because you lived it or loved someone who has.

This is my journey out of the jails, institutions, and (potential) death that is promised when we are trapped in the drug world. A firsthand account of the road less traveled toward victory over addiction. We'll visit the rehabs, the homeless shelters and the hospitals. We'll touch on the times I slipped up and the times I stood firm. We'll stand in front of judges and in front of pastors. We'll talk about what it really takes to rebuild a life from the ground up, to leave behind selfish survival and step into a life of service and purpose. There are stories of loss and of love, separation and restoration, and the path toward redemption and finally healing.

I have changed or omitted the names of many of my friends and, to further protect their anonymity, I have left out the name of the small California town where we resided. I share this story as I remember it, with details as clearly stated as possible. Some details have been slightly changed or omitted for further protection and some conversations/ characters have been condensed. Others may remember it differently, but they are welcome to write their own story.

Interwoven throughout the book is an opportunity for you to dig into your own history, with teachings and reflective questions to help you dig a little deeper into what it is that may be keeping you stuck. I hope you will use them as a tool to look within yourself for a truer understanding of who you are, why you may do the things you do and how to stop the thing you don't like doing, but can't seem to give up. I couldn't imagine writing a whole book that is only about me, so I made space for you too. My one thing was drugs, but yours can be anything; shopping, porn, alcohol, gambling, food, sex, fill in the blank. Chances are that you know what your one thing is.

I am no one special. I don't seek accolades or applause for finally living the life that I should have lived from the start. But I do have a heart for those of you who haven't figured it out yet, and those of you who don't believe you ever will. I have this deep-rooted desire to hold the flashlight for you while you find your way out of the darkness you've been trapped in, just like someone held the light for me. I believe in you during the times that you can't even fathom believing in yourself, because if I can get out, so can you.

Do you feel that tug? Do you hear a still, small voice telling you to turn the page? I hope the story written in these pages gives you a better un-derstanding of a life ravaged by addiction. I hope you read these pages and finally see that there is a way out. I hope that you are encouraged and inspired to step out of your own comfort zone and into something more. I hope that you will find your own story within these pages. And I hope above all, that you find a little faith in the greatest power of all between these two covers.

See you on the other side.

With hope,

Chapter 1

Learning the Hard Way

"The burned hand teaches best.
After that, advice about fire goes to the heart."

~ J.R.R Tolkien

BANG–Clink.

The giant metal doors slammed shut behind me, and the familiar click of the locks engaging echoed through the dorm.

"Harris, Cell 6," came over the loudspeaker. I made my way towards the door of my suicide watch cell, carrying my green mat, grey wool blanket, and t-shirt-nightgown.

It was the middle of the night, and the dorm was quiet. My faceless bunkie rolled over from her bottom bunk long enough for me to see that I had disturbed her dreams of someplace far better than her reality. She groaned and went back to sleep. I couldn't see her face and didn't know who she was, or if we'd be able to get along, but right then, I had little desire to think about her.

I had just spent the last seven hours sitting at the police station, being dragged to the county jail in the back of a cop car, sitting in the reception cell as I called bail bondsmen on a whim (with no luck), meeting with the physician and the psychiatrist, being fully strip-searched and physically inspected, and begging my friend who hadn't been arrested to put money on my books with one of my free calls.

I was starting to feel the onset of withdrawal symptoms hitting my bones. The fatigue was ready to pounce on me at any given second. So, I climbed up onto my top bunk, tried to get comfortable on the paper-thin mat, and dozed off.

It felt like I'd been asleep for maybe fifteen minutes when the lights came blaring on above me. The bang of cell doors opening all around the dorm startled me awake. I woke up confused, momentarily having forgotten that I was, once again, waking up in the county jail. I paused for a moment after opening my eyes, staring at the ceiling as I contemplated whether or not to get up at all.

Eventually I decided that missing a meal when I was about to shift into physical detox was probably not the best idea. I climbed off my top bunk and made my way out into the chow line. The menu today had lukewarm coffee, pre-cut orange slices and oatmeal that had been sitting long enough for a milky skin to form over the top of it. Breakfast of criminal champions.

I glanced around, searching for familiar faces. The room held the usual cast of characters you'd expect to see during that first stop in county jail. There were the comfortable ones—women like me who were likely repeat offenders. We already knew the routine and how to quietly pass the time until we received our housing assignment. Then there were the criers, probably here for only their first or second visit, wrapped in that heavy blanket of defeat that settles over you when the reality hits that you're actually in jail. And, as always, a line of anxious girls stretched along the brick wall, each one clinging to the phone or waiting for their turn, desperate to find a way out.

Eventually, I spotted Marissa, the young girl who'd been in the car with me the night before. I think it's pretty standard in any jail for everyone to go to suicide watch for the first three days so the cops in the security bubble can keep a closer eye on the new residents. They also spend that time deciding which housing pod we'll be sent to next. I was a red-and-black band classification, which meant that I wasn't quite angry or violent enough to be a red-bander—those inmates are locked down 23 hours per day—but I'd had enough disciplinary reports during my visits here to not qualify for a white band like the rest of general population. White-banders were granted a bit more freedom while outside of their cells.

Marissa came gliding over to me at my cell door, appearing completely unbothered by her current situation.

"What time did you get here?" She asked.

"I don't know. Late. What'd they end up bringing you in for?"

"Warrants. They're not for nothing crazy so I'll probably just see the judge and get out. No new charges. What about you?"

"They charged me with transportation of narcotics. The cop took me to the station to see how much there was and it was over two pounds so he said he had no choice. But it's only pot–how bad can a pot charge really be?" I said.

"Oh yeah, weed ain't nothin. You'll be fine." She turned and walked away as another young girl I knew rushed over, looking frazzled and stressed.

"Girl, I'm so glad you're here. I need you to take something! You can sell it if you want, but I can't have it on me in here, I'll get caught or beat up or something," she yell-whispered, leaning in closer to my face.

I instantly and instinctively knew what it was that she was so desperate to hide.

The fact that the bag of meth hadn't been found during the search of her body was a miracle, but I had no idea what to do with it now that we were inside. Getting busted with drugs in a jail facility was probably a massive charge, and needed to be avoided at all costs. I could have taken it and flushed it, but what a waste! I considered selling it like she said, but the currency in there consisted of snickers bars and honey buns. I could have taken it and done it, but I had no desire whatsoever to be high on meth in a concrete jungle like that.

So instead, with no real plan, I unscrewed my shampoo bottle, poured most of it out (I was sure I'd regret that later), and shoved the bag of drugs into it. I went back into my cell, put it under my mattress, and went back to sleep, still in my county-jail blues. I would spend at least the next week coming down, which pretty much meant deep sleep and body aches. I'd been awake for about eight days before getting arrested, so my body was completely drained. I drifted off quickly.

Kicking drugs in jail was never easy. I'd been poisoning my body with a plethora of downers: opiates, black tar heroin, weed... But I'd also had enough amphetamines to keep a body builder awake for a week. The combination of the two created some confusion inside of me, where I yearned for sleep from the constant stimulation but had to fight the nausea as the opiates left my system.

My skin ached, my eyes felt heavy and like they'd recently been set on fire, and the muscles in my legs and arms cramped sporadically while I slept. Luckily, I needed the sleep so badly that I spent most of the next few days passed out, waking up only long enough to hit the chow line and take a few bites of the trash they called food. I was mostly emotionless about my arrest, especially during those first few days. I had been to jail enough times to not really feel phased by it anymore. By this point, the arrests had become so frequent that I'd begun to look at them as more of a temporary reprieve from the streets than as an actual punishment for the laws I'd been breaking. I would take my three hot meals and a cot to sleep on and allow myself to rest and reset before going back out into the world to do it all over again.

Around midday on the third day, a voice came over the loudspeaker advising me that I had court that afternoon for my arraignment. Finally, I'd have an idea of how long I'd be here this time. Going to court felt like an all-day process, and on some occasions, it was. The voice in the ceiling would alert us an hour before it was time to leave. Then we were escorted down a long hallway in a straight line.

They say the color blue is supposed to promote a sense of calmness, so every inch of the hallway was blue, including the stripe that the inmates kept their shoulders against as we walked with our hands behind our backs. There was a pit stop along the way where inmates kneeled on boxes as officers tightened shackles around our ankles before shuffling us to an all-brown holding cell to await our turn in front of the judge.

Once our name was called, we were brought into the courtroom, with the general public blockaded from us by a chain link fence. The separation between the caged criminal and the average person was unmistakable. If someone cared about or loved the criminal on the other side of the fence enough, you wouldn't have to stay there very long. Bail would likely be paid for you. But if you're unwanted or unloved, if no one chooses to take you home, you maintain your spot in the cage. I imagine this is the same feeling a dog in a kennel might experience while waiting for a family to adopt them. *Please let there be a nice family out there that will find me a bail bondsman who takes promises instead of money*, I thought to myself.

I was staring blankly out at the courtroom, sitting amongst the other arrestees in our matching orange t-shirts and light blue jumpsuits, when someone standing at the gate called my name. I'd had this same public defender before. She was a woman of small stature with mousy brown hair cut short, wearing a pantsuit that looked too big for her tiny frame.

"Back again, Harris?" she asked.

I shrugged and gave her a look that I hoped conveyed that I wasn't in the mood for lectures. I was still coming down and was slightly worried about the shampoo bottle I'd left stashed under the mattress in my cell.

"So, the DA is charging you with transportation of marijuana, a felony. The offer on the table if you plead guilty today is two years. I think you should take it."

"*Two years?*" I asked, the surprise impossible to hide from my voice. "It was just weed! I'm not a drug trafficker."

"It was more than two pounds of weed in a moving vehicle broken out into separate containers. That's a drug trafficker in the eyes of the law. Not to mention that this is your twelfth arrest in four years. You're already on felony probation and six informal probations. You'll have to do ninety days at least for those violations. If you take the deal, you'll get double credits while you're here. You'll be out in fifteen months."

"That's insane. Fifteen months in prison is insane! What about drug court?" I asked.

"You've already maxed out all your strikes with drug court." She calmly looked down at the file in her hand.

"How does that last rehab even count? I was only there for like a week."

"You jumped out the window of their disciplinary room. That isn't the act of someone who wants to get clean."

"They left me in that room by myself for six hours. If being in an empty room for six hours is how people get clean, then wouldn't jail have worked by now? I'm not taking the deal."

"I strongly advise you to take the deal. If you take it to trial and lose, the amount of time you get could double."

"Not guilty," I said sternly.

"You told the arresting officer that it was yours."

"But I wasn't even driving. Not guilty."

"Okay, have a seat and wait for your name," she said, with obvious frustration in her voice.

By the time the judge called my name, my mind was reeling. But I stood up calmly and walked to the small microphone that stood in front of the gate.

"Please state your full name for the court," the judge said.

I did.

"Ms. Harris, you're being charged with felony transportation of two pounds of marijuana in a moving vehicle. How do you plead?"

"Not guilty, sir," I replied, sounding a lot more timid than I'd intended to.

"Very well. You are remanded to the custody of the jail until your next court date. Bail is revoked for recommendations of probation violations and court is set for thirty days from today."

And that was that.

As I waited in the holding cell to be taken back to the dorms, my thoughts ranged from how unfair the judicial system is, to how mad I was that I'd taken the full blame for all that weed, to wondering if fifteen months in prison was actually the best I was going to get.

People came and went from that small brown room. Officers coming to collect inmates that had already been seen by the judge, inmates waiting for their turn in the cage, inmates like me who had already been seen and now sat contemplatively, sporadically releasing sighs and groans of frustration. I barely even noticed them. Instead, I replayed the actions from the past week over and over again in my mind. Technically it was my weed in the back of that car—even though it hadn't started out that way.

I'd met a guy who gave me a ride, and somehow we ended up back at his house getting high. He was your average-looking tweeker, skinny and scrawny with sharp movements and tense gestures that made his body look like it was made out of metal instead of flesh. When we got to his room, he opened his cupboards to reveal shelves full of jars of weed. Come to find out, he had stolen the car he'd been driving from the president of the local chapter of a notorious biker crew's son, and the six pounds of weed in the trunk was just a happy surprise.

He wasn't sure what he was going to do with it all, but within minutes, I'd concocted a plan to take it from him. Show up, act tough, bring someone tougher than him to stand behind me, and watch as it was all handed over.

It wasn't difficult to take things from druggies if you showed up with a mean-enough looking dude. In the end, the guy actually helped us put the jars into duffle bags and carried it out to the car for us. He handed me the keys to the stolen car and said "No hard feelings. It was fun while it lasted." It was the easiest theft that I'd ever been a part of.

Originally, my plan was to give everything back to the rightful owner and earn a few points with the powerful group of bikers. So, I called the president of said biker crew and told him that I'd found the car and would meet his son to return it. But Junior had a bad attitude. When he came to get the car, he snatched me up by the shirt, demanding his pot be returned as he called me a dirty, tweeker whore. I'd never been too good at recognizing when the situation I was in might be a little dangerous, so it was second nature for me to laugh in his face and tell him, "Looks like you just got burnt."

Luckily, that same mean dude was there to step between us, or that conversation may have ended even worse than it did.

Fast forward to a few days later, and I had jars of weed spread out in closets all over the city. It was the only option I could come up with. Being homeless makes it tough to hide anything, especially drugs. But as we were driving the last of the weed to a different hiding place, those familiar red-and-blue lights began to flash behind us. Which brings us back to the current scenario, where I could potentially spend two years in prison for weed that I stole from a tweeker, who stole it from a biker gang.

REFLECT

The choices I made in life up to this point lacked serious evaluation. My life had become a series of reckless decisions and preventable outcomes, where the path I took often resulted in prolonged jail time. I lived my life on a quest for one thing: the getting and having of whatever I wanted in that moment. The physical need for more drugs outweighed everything else. The mental stronghold of survival had me in its grips. Any sense of responsibility to myself or others paled in comparison to that.

I was often ill-prepared for the consequences of my decisions. Whether I was facing the repercussions of a biker crew or a judge, I rarely thought through anything long enough to envision the direction that my next move could take me in. I had to learn things the hard way because that was the only way I ever learned anything at all.

For much of my life, I'd been able to slide through some of these more stressful moments without any real punishment. My surprise at a potential prison term makes this clear—I never expected that the crime I committed would result in an actual long-term consequence. Sometimes the lessons we are taught in life fall directly in line with whether we are able to identify an unsafe situation when we are approaching it. Without the hard lessons, we often lack the knowledge we need to avoid similar instances in the future.

There was another side to me, though. There was the side of me that would take full blame for the marijuana even though I wasn't driving the car and could have let the driver take the fault. The side that took the hidden drugs from my young friend because she was afraid, despite the risk it created for me. In some ways, those two decisions show a very different piece of my character. It was a constant battle that seemed to rage inside me: the desire to do and be good against what felt like a physical inability to see it through. The good versus the bad, the moral versus the immoral, the honest person versus the liar. Which side would win on any given day was usually a surprise, even to me.

I would wager that most of us are like this, just maybe faced with less extreme circumstances. We are complex people, with thoughts and feelings that we have to navigate through every day. When we couple that complexity with a dependency on some outside thing like drugs, we often lead ourselves into destructive patterns and uncertain results. We all take risks every day of our lives, but some of us just don't know when we've taken a few too many.

REFLECTIVE QUESTIONS

1. Quick decisions are a part of life, but they don't always work out how we think they will. Describe a time when you made a snap decision and then had to face unexpected consequences.

    _____

    _____

    _____

    _____

2. How do you define recklessness? By your own definition, would you consider yourself reckless? Why or why not?

    _____

    _____

    _____

    _____

3. We all have complex traits that shape who we are. Do you ever feel like two sides of yourself are in conflict? If so, is there a side that usually wins?

    _____

    _____

    _____

    _____

Chapter 2
Sitting in a Cage

"In spite of how things may appear to us, we are never trapped by where we are. The trap is always who we are."

~ Guy Finley

As soon as I came back from court for the stolen drugs, the voice in the speaker piped up and commanded that I get my stuff ready to be re-housed. I slowly made my way out of suicide watch and into the pod right next door. I still had a shampoo bottle full of meth tucked safely inside my bra. My heart pounded in my chest as I picked up my things and walked into what would be my home for the foreseeable future, with an officer following close behind.

The woman sitting in my new cell had long, wavy red hair and a cheerful disposition. I liked her right away, which was a welcome change from the cell mates I'd had in the past. They ranged from a yellow-bander (psych inmate) who tried to slit her wrists in the middle of the night with a stolen razor, to a pilates instructor who never sat down for longer than a few minutes at a time, to an older woman with viciously poor hygiene whose constant odor seemed to hang on the walls, to a Hispanic woman who didn't speak a word of English and had committed a crime while in the US illegally. Eventually, the ICE team barged into our cell to take her away.

My new bunkie had already been in that cell for a few months and only had about six weeks left of her sentence before she'd be released back into the real world. Within the first few days, I revealed to her that I had brought more into our cell than my sleepy disposition and withdrawal symptoms and, of course, she wanted to partake.

I couldn't wrap my head around the idea that people actually wanted to be high on meth in jail. Pills or heroin I could understand, because you could just sleep your time away, but staying awake all night listening to the officers walk past our cell hourly, click the little counter button onto the door, and peek in the window made no sense to me. But, I didn't want to hold onto this stuff forever, so I proceeded to let her have some of it. She proceeded to share it with other women in the pod on our Day Room cycle.

During all of my various trips to jail, I was kept in the six-hour program. Which meant for six hours out of the day, the downstairs cells had Day Room and for the other six hours, the upstairs did, alternating morning and afternoon shifts. The rest of the time was spent in our cells, occupying our time as best we could with limited activities. You'd be amazed at how quickly you can read the *Twilight* saga when you're locked in a room for twenty four hours every other day. You'd also be surprised how many hardened criminals are willing to fight for their turn with the *Twilight* Saga, but we won't get into that right now.

As news traveled swiftly amongst the inmates that there was dope in the facility, I secretly became everyone's best friend and newfound hero. People slid candy bars and honey buns to me from across the table, as I'd predicted, and gave me phone time without me even having to ask. Before I knew it, the dope was almost gone and the whole pod was high except for maybe the little old lady in cell number two and me.

The cops must have become suspicious of the lack of sleep going on and the excessive drawing, card-playing and general happiness in our pod, because they decided to raid it. Both levels of the jail had been placed on lockdown for our after lunch "quiet time"—aka shift change—when suddenly all the doors banged open. At least twenty officers flooded in, and the voice over the loudspeaker ordered everyone out of their cells and into the Day Room for body searches.

To say that I was in sheer panic mode is the understatement of the century. My whole body shook as I was shoved against the wall by the hulk. The hulk was a butch female officer, her blonde hair always pulled back in a low half-knot, who was popular with the lesbian and "gay for the stay" inmates—those who are straight in the free world but, for any number of reasons, change their status when not. She wasn't mean per se, but she was definitely the toughest female officer in that jail.

"Why are you so nervous?" she asked as her gloved hands patted me down, reached up my shirt, and ran under my sports bra elastic.

"I dunno, when was the last time you were shoved against a wall and felt up by another woman?" I asked, trying to sound calm through my quivering voice.

She shrugged, gave me a look that conveyed she understood my discomfort, and moved along with her search.

After she had finished searching me and shifted me to another wall, I glanced nervously up at my cell, just waiting for the ominous shampoo bottle to be tossed down and for my cell mate and I to be taken to see the sergeant for our punishment and my new charges. But somehow, that didn't happen. They moved on from my cell to the next. The only contraband they found were a few razors that had been snuck in by the worker inmates, dice made out of toilet paper that we used to play Yahtzee and sanitary pads that we'd make-shifted into tampons.

When we went back into our now trashed cell, I searched for the shampoo bottle. Low and behold, it was still there, and so was the bag of crystals, tucked safely inside.

At that moment, I decided the risk was not worth the commissary or phone cards, so I pulled the bag out and flushed it, to my bunkie's absolute horror.

I had never felt more relieved than I was when I had finally gotten rid of the remaining drugs. I didn't feel vindicated by not being caught, I felt stupid, knowing that I probably should have flushed it all from day one. My street mentality wouldn't allow me to release something I knew was dangerous to have, forcing me to take even more unnecessary risk. Once the stress of my secret was no longer weighing me down, the time began to pass again in the way it usually does when you're enclosed in the same place for a while.

I can't tell you if time spent in jail feels like it moves faster or slower than time spent in the real world. It almost feels as if it stands completely still. You know the rest of the world is existing as it always has, and people are living their lives out there as they've always done, but the absence of reality starts to become normal, and your existence becomes just a mundane routine that you slowly get used to. But there are pieces of your humanity that slowly chip away the longer you sit in a cage.

Being in jail was nothing new to me. It had become just another part of my life that fit perfectly with the rest. I'd been homeless for a long time by this point, moving from couch to couch in the home of whichever person would let me in. I would usually wear out my welcome after a while and need to move on. In between couches, I occasionally spent nights in a tent at the river bottom or under a freeway overpass with the more permanently homeless population. I can't even tell you how many times I've stayed in empty or abandoned houses, hijacking a hose from the neighbor to flush the toilet or hooking up a small, probably stolen, generator for a little electricity. On some occasions, I'd stay awake and hang out on the top level of a parking garage at the promenade near the beach. If there was ever any extra money, I'd stay in Motel 6 for a few days and pretend I was on vacation. I was a wanderer, a gypsy, a nomad. And as long as I had some kind of drug to keep me moving, I was mostly okay with the way I lived.

Once I began to feel normal again and the withdrawal had mostly subsided, I pulled together enough courage to call my mom and tell her that things weren't looking too good for me. I'd called from the holding tank when I first arrived, but this call would prove to be much harder to get through.

"Hi Kels," she said, after the robotic voice had finished asking her if she'd accept the call.

"Hey Mom. I'm still here."

"I figured. When I didn't hear from you for a while, I looked up your case online. What's the deal this time?" she asked.

"I'm not sure yet. It's just a weed charge, but I think I've run out of chances. I'm not too sure how long I'm gonna be here, but I decided not to plead guilty right away." I'm sure the shame in my voice was clear, but I tried to sound strong. I didn't want her to worry, though I was pretty sure that by now, she worried less when I was in jail than she did when I wasn't.

"Well, I talked with your son's counselor. We decided since he's seven years old now that it would be best to tell him the truth about where you are this time. Telling him you left California to visit Las Vegas again doesn't seem fair anymore. He took it okay—we kind of talked about it like you're in time out."

Tears welled up in my eyes as I thought about my baby knowing that his mommy was in jail and wouldn't be seeing him for a while.

"I understand. Can I talk to him?" I asked.

"Of course," she said.

"Hi Mommy!"

"Hi Carter! I miss you so much, bubba. Are you being good?"

"I miss you too. Yes, I'm being good. Gramma said you got in trouble and you had to go to timeout."

"Yeah, baby, I got in trouble. That's why being a good boy is so important."

"I know. Do you have to wear black and white stripes?"

"No baby, I'm wearing blue and orange. But it's not stripes," I said, trying to stop myself from choking up.

For some reason, the innocence of that question seemed to break through my tough exterior, and I started to fall apart a little. I knew if I cried, he would cry, and I couldn't let him hear that I was holding in tears.

"Can I talk to Gramma again bubba? I love you so much, and I'll call again soon."

"Yeah, love you too!"

"Hello? That was quick," my mom said.

"I know, I couldn't hold it together. I've gotta go Mom. I'll call you again when I can," I said, with sobs ready to erupt at any second.

"Ok, talk to you soon." Click.

I turned from the payphone and swallowed my sobs, relaxing my face. The last thing I was gonna do was let the rest of the pod see me cry. Pain wasn't for the surface. I had learned to hold it deep inside over the years, if I ever even felt it at all anymore.

I had actually been pretty sensitive when I was young, with emotions too big and intense for my small mind to comprehend. I was also curious and a little nosy. My dad often said that I was the type of kid that needed to touch the fire myself to see if it was actually hot, no matter how many times he tried to warn me that I'd be burned. That ideology became a refrain in my life for many years to come. I never trusted the warnings or advice of others. I needed first-hand experience and believed that only by directly engaging with something would I fully understand what I was told about it. The trust issues ran deep, even from childhood.

Dad was a drug addict. He was angry a lot, and we never knew from one day to the next if he would be the funny, happy dad or the screaming, yelling dad. Mom seemed to be around less and less the older we got. She started working in a casino overnight while he struggled to hold down a job. Later, she would seek comfort in pouring the family money into the chiming video poker machines to avoid the abuse in our house. It only ever seemed to make things worse in the long run.

Her gambling and his anger would impact every area of our young lives. She often sat at the slot machines in the grocery store throwing away countless dollars while we waited for her in the magazine section. We would look for her in the mornings after her graveyard shift only to find that she'd stayed at the casino well past her scheduled hours to gamble her tips. The fights that her financial manipulations created would echo throughout our childhood home as the rage spilled out of our father. His angry outbursts would often result in smashed dishes and destroyed keepsakes all over the kitchen floor. These outbursts would affect us the most during our formative years, though we wouldn't realize how bad they really were until much later.

The early years though, were quiet and calm. Dad traveled around the world, working as a stage manager for big names like the Rolling Stones, Jackson 5, and Reba McEntire. Mom kept a handle on things back home until baby number three arrived, when he made the decision to retire from the music industry and come back home. He traded in a life of rock stars and road trips for one of Barbie dolls and ballet recitals, usually working with his brother on fancy hotel remodels for income.

My two sisters and I learned to navigate through a home where we were always on edge, never certain of what kind of experience we would have from one day to the next. As the middle daughter, I experienced some of those cliche feelings of not fitting in or feeling forgotten or left out. Some days I felt like an old toy that you'd find in the back of the closet—the one you only take out to play with when you can't think of anything else to do. After a while, I found my own ways to get off the shelf and out in the world.

I experienced an unspoken pain that seemed to deepen as I got older, a dull ache that just existed within me. I questioned if anyone actually liked me and struggled to keep friends for very long. My tendency to latch on to one friend at a time and spend so much time in their home to escape having to be in my own would cause me to quickly wear out my welcome. I'd be forced to move from friend to friend frequently.

There was Sheila, a small-for-her-age ginger tomboy who broke her arm more than once playing baseball. As her interest in sports grew, I tried to keep up but failed. My chubby little body couldn't do the same things that hers could. There was also Alisha, the freckled girl scout who stopped hanging out with me when I told her that my dad sometimes called me the B-word. She surprised me when she said her daddy only ever called her *princess*. And there was Misty, her long hair reaching down past the joints in her skinny knees. Her timid approach to things made our friendship last the longest. But when we started junior high, she shifted over to the smart-kid group, and I found other types of friends. I never felt as athletic, or as loved, or as smart as these girls, and those feelings of not being good enough seemed to increase the older I became. So eventually, I sought out friends who would help me find ways to stop the painful feelings I didn't want anymore.

Growing up in Las Vegas, it wasn't unusual to start snorting meth at thirteen years old that you had procured from men well in their twenties or older. My father's angry and often violent nature had pushed me to find these outlets away from home. The drug world accepted me and always provided a place of escape, with new friends who didn't care how long I stayed or if I actually fit in with them. And the drugs made me feel… well, they made me feel nothing. And that's how I liked it.

For the most part, my drug and I grew up together. We were the best of friends, and it was always there for me when I needed it. It was by my side at all the monumental moments that mark a teenager's life: getting my driver's license, my first fight, my first kiss, going to school each day—that is, until I dropped out on the third day of junior year, but it was there for me during that time too. My drug was with me for all of it, and it provided me with a comfortable numbness that I needed in order to exist in the world that I had barely been able to stumble through.

Finding out I was pregnant at barely nineteen years old left me confused, somewhere between excited about having a little human to love and terrified that I would turn this little human into another version of me. I was six years deep into a meth addiction by this point and living with my divorced mother in Las Vegas, where the chaos of my life often followed me home. I frequented shady trailer parks and sleazy motel rooms. My best friends were meth cooks and drug traffickers. There was violence lurking around most corners. I had guns and dope hidden in multiple spaces in my bedroom. I was incapable of functioning without a daily dose of the drug that kept me going and could barely take care of myself, let alone another person who would need to rely solely on me for survival. Teenage pregnancy is challenging enough, but add in an addictive lifestyle and it's practically impossible.

My child's father told me he didn't want to participate in raising him, and I fell into a deep depression. I had considered ending the pregnancy. I randomly got up one day to drive myself to a clinic. I didn't even know what the clinic was called—I didn't know anything about abortion, but I knew even less about being a single teenage mom.

I think driving in the car that day was the first time I ever prayed. I asked for a sign—am I doing the right thing? Is this decision a one-way ticket to addiction absolution? Will I ever recover from this? And, as I breathed out the last few words of a broken prayer, an Amanda Perez song came on the radio, *God Send Me an Angel*.

"God send me an angel, from the heavens above.
Send me an angel to heal my broken heart,
From being in love.
'Cause all I do is cry
God, send me an angel
To wipe the tears from my eyes"

I pulled over, cried for a while, and then drove home. Somewhere in this moment, the question of whether or not I was keeping my baby was answered. Not knowing what would happen, how things would work out, or if I'd be a good mom, I decided to try.

On an autumn afternoon a few months later, I gave birth to my son in a small kiddie pool in the living room, with a midwife. I was surrounded by at least a dozen family and friends, all with tears in their eyes as my little boy entered the world. I loved him the moment I saw him. He was perfect: 8lbs, 13oz., a full head of dark hair, and the most beautiful little eyes I had ever seen.

But, and it kills me to say this, my love for him was overpowered by the pain I still felt inside. Within only a few days I was back with my drug, attempting to feel normal again so I could care for this new life that I'd brought into the world.

REFLECT

Standing against that brick wall, waiting for my new punishment, elicited a level of fear in me that is hard to imagine. As someone who didn't experience fear very often in my addiction, this feeling was strange. Why was I willing to risk more of my freedom for a bag of drugs I had no intention of even doing? And why was I the only addict in the room who didn't want to use them?

I found new questions to ask about myself that day: was I more addicted to the way the rest of the inmates viewed me, and what I could get from them, than I was to the drug itself? The risks I took were often based on my own self-value. And the less I valued myself, the riskier my life would become.

Sitting in a cage built up walls inside me that reached far higher than the walls that physically surrounded me. Each brick represented a part of me that I couldn't let anyone see. When we blockade ourselves from tough emotions, we never really learn the lesson that these experiences are trying to teach us. It is often the act of feeling our own pain that leads us to make the decision to pause before taking another risk and facing negative consequences over and over. If we never allow ourselves to feel that pain, we forget that the consequences may be harmful.

Many of us don't realize that the experiences we have as children directly impact what type of adults we become. The things we believe about ourselves at a young age can follow us well into adolescence and eventually adulthood, helping to determine our self-esteem and thought patterns. I believed that most people didn't want me around for very long, which created feelings of rejection and unworthiness. Those feelings followed me for a very long time.

Regardless of how vastly I would eventually mess up, choosing life for my son, against all odds and with no plan or idea of how it would turn out, ended up being the greatest decision I've ever made. He has always been the best piece of me and the purest form of love I've ever experienced. Sometimes we get the chance to briefly hold onto something without knowing how long we will get to hold it. But the time we do get is precious and often worth the pain we may eventually endure.

REFLECTIVE QUESTIONS

1. We take risks everyday, but there is usually a line that marks just how far we are willing to go. What do you think it means to base risk levels on self-worth? Can you relate to that idea?

_____

_____

_____

_____

2. It's natural to want to feel protected, but sometimes our effort to shield ourselves from pain goes too far. What kinds of emotional walls do you think you put up? What do you feel these walls are protecting you from?

_____

_____

_____

_____

3. Have you ever prayed for clarity and felt like you got an immediate answer? If so, what was that experience like?

_____

_____

_____

_____

Chapter 3
Chasing Freedom

*"Better to die fighting for freedom, than be a prisoner
all the days of your life."*

~ Bob Marley

After I pleaded not guilty at my initial court date, my defense went into full swing. What that meant for me was… basically nothing. I continued to hang out in the rooms made of concrete while the public defender attempted to find any semblance of a reason that the prosecution should choose not to send me to prison. Each time she visited me, we would cover the same topic in circles, always with the same outcome. She wanted me to take the deal, and I didn't.

The progress with my case was at a total standstill. The court dates showed up every four weeks like clockwork. I'd make the same journey down the long blue hall, stopping at the box for ankle shackles, sitting in the brown cell with forty other inmates while waiting for my name to be called, with little to no change in the situation. At the end of each visit, they'd hand me a stack of yellow papers that pretty much summed up what had taken place in the courtroom. A whole bunch of nothing, and a dollar amount at the bottom for what I owed for each endeavor. With each visit, I watched that number slowly increase.

Once I had finally come down from all the drugs I'd been taking before my arrest, insomnia followed the lethargy. It didn't help matters that a small ceiling light stayed on twenty-four hours a day, so that the officer doing rounds could always see exactly what was happening on the top and bottom bunks. I'd often try to cover it with paper or cardboard from the back of a notepad from the commissary. Inevitably, the overnight officer would tap on the cell door with a small flashlight and tell me to take it down. Once that happened, all bets were off that I'd catch any real sleep.

I sat in the Day Room one afternoon during our six hours of social interaction via card playing, television-watching, and threading each other's eyebrows with a string pulled from the county issued orange socks we all possessed. I started to complain about my sleep situation. Or lack thereof.

"Why don't you tell the psych that you have anxiety? They'll give you some meds."

It was common practice on the inside for every girl to come up with as many excuses as she could muster to hear her name shouted out at Pill Call. If she was an addict, she'd sometimes have multiple calls a day. Other girls would sell the pills they got by cheeking them and spitting them back out into a tissue. No one cared about the common concerns we think of on the outside. We had to use the toilet in front of each other in the middle of our bedroom, so what's the harm in a little spit?

"Hey, come here." One of the inmates from across the Day Room waved me over.

She was one of the shot-callers in the pod—though that title was considered common knowledge more often than it was ever spoken out loud—a Hispanic lesbian with long black hair that she wore slicked back into a low braid. We all knew that she was high up in a street gang, and she required a certain level of respect. But from my perspective, she was funny and laid-back, and she liked to crack jokes and hit on all the younger girls that came in who didn't know exactly how a jail stay worked. I wasn't intimidated by her, and it would be years before I questioned if maybe I should have been.

"Hey, I get meds for sleep like every night, and I don't want 'em. You want 'em?" she asked.

"Yeah, I do. But I don't have money on my books or anything. I don't really have anybody to hook me up on the outside."

"Girl, I don't want your money. Just have my back in here, and I'll have yours. We look out for each other. I'll help you get some sleep."

I agreed. I knew why she chose to help me. I'd always been known as a fighter and a bully. I wore a tough face and lacked the ability to walk away when any negative emotion was triggered. I almost always chose violence to settle any issues, and that reputation seemed to precede me. I was still surprised that she didn't want any money, and I figured that it would cost me in some other way eventually, but I was so desperate for sleep that it didn't really matter.

I'll admit that the pills she got every night were strong. I slept like a baby, and I only had to take one of the two she'd give me every morning, wrapped in toilet paper. I don't know how she did it, but she'd keep the pills looking shiny and new every time. You could still see the identifying number-letter combo etched into the white. I'd store the extra pills in the same notorious shampoo bottle that had proven itself quite useful already.

I was able to rest in sweet, medicated bliss for a few weeks before the familiar sound of the doors banging open and the squad of correctional officers flooded the dorm. They yelled at us to get up and step out of our cells for a search. Great.

Standing with my forehead pressed against the brick wall again, I doubted I would be as lucky as I was the first time this happened. But still had my fingers crossed that the shampoo bottle would make it through one more time. Time passed slowly as they went cell to cell collecting contraband, until they started to call out the names of those who would be faced with disciplinary action for whatever they'd discovered. We all held our breath.

"Garcia and Michaels, cell four. Houston and Gundry, cell eight. Diaz and Thomspon, cell 11. Harris and Ruiz, cell 14."

The two of us from my cell were to be advised of what was found and either take personal responsibility, and only one would face repercussions, or we'd both be punished for the item. As we walked upstairs to our current home, all I could see was a giant man in uniform with a small shampoo bottle in his hand.

———

"Okay, Harris, you've been charged with possession of contraband in the form of medication not prescribed to you. How do you plead?"

The sergeant was an older gentleman, his face weathered from all the years of handing out punishments to a bunch of adults who didn't know how to function like normal people. There was a hardness and a gentleness to him at the same time, but it was easy to tell that he was a no-nonsense kind of guy.

"Guilty."

"Would you like to tell me who this medication is actually prescribed to and avoid some time in solitary?" he asked, with his head down and his eyes looking up at me from over the rim of his reading glasses.

"No, sir."

"Didn't think so. By your admission, we find you guilty of the charges against you. Your punishment will be as follows: fourteen days no commissary or phone time and five days spent in disciplinary segregation. Here's a list of the items you're allowed to bring with you, and we'll keep the rest of your belongings stored for you until the days are completed, at which time you'll be moved to a different housing pod. Understood?" He sounded like he had spoken these exact words thousands of times to thousands of inmates.

"Understood"

I looked down at the list that the sergeant handed me in the hallway of the county jail.

Sleeping mat

Blanket

Towel

Paper

Pencils

Religious books

This wasn't the first time I'd been sent to the hole, but it would be the longest.

I'm sure most people imagine the hole to be dark and silent, and that's probably how it is in a lot of places, but here it was the exact opposite. At this jail, solitary was a long hallway of ten one-man cells, five on each side. The lights stay on all day and night, so you never knew what time it was or how long you've been there. Randomly throughout the day, an officer came to escort us one at a time to take a five-minute shower. We'd all lean sharply against the door to try and see out of the four-by-four-inch window that was covered by a small curtain, trying to tie a face to a voice we'd been listening to for hours or catch a glimpse of a real window to see if it was night or day. Because the ceiling lights never went out, no one ever slept. The echoes of each woman yelling to the woman in the cell next to or across from her were constant.

We all did our fair share of reading on the inside, and having to go five days without a book felt like the worst part of being in solitary. I brought a Bible with me and the other permitted items on the list. As my name was called to begin the long walk out of my cell and into the next five days of isolation, I felt the dread of knowing I was walking into the better part of a week of sleeplessness and boredom.

The time passed by slowly, as I had suspected it would. I watched through the crack under the door as girls fished kites (notes) to each other from one cell to the next using a long string from their sock or t-shirt. I didn't have the patience to pull out a long enough string, and I didn't have the desire to read or write a kite to a stranger in another cell, so I stayed out of this daily game that was played for hours on end and kept to myself.

I opened that Bible multiple times and tried to read it from the beginning. I'd get to the part where Cain killed Abel, then all the genealogies would start, and I'd lose interest. I can't even tell you how many times I read the story of creation in that little room, but it lost my attention or went over my head at the same spot every time.

I'm not sure what made me decide to try reading a different part of the Bible, but one day, I opened to the book of Romans and started there. It was all about the law—breaking it, following it, and who we are without it. The words seemed to jump off the page—being justified by the law, being judged by the law. Today, I know that Paul was writing about biblical law, but at the time I felt like he was talking about me, my court case, my desire to fight a charge that I knew I was guilty of, my inherent selfishness and rebellion against the law. Each word spoke to me and to my wicked heart, telling me that I was trying to force an outcome I didn't deserve. I deserved prison.

Then I came to Romans 7:15.

"I do not understand what I do. For what I want to do I do not do, but what I hate, I do. And if I do what I do not want to do, I agree that the law is good. As it is, it is no longer myself who do it, but it is sin living in me. For I know that good itself does not dwell in me, that is, in my sinful nature. For I have the desire to do what is good, but I cannot carry it out. For I do not do the good I want to do, but the evil I do not want to do—this I keep doing. Now if I do what I do not want to do, it is no longer I who do it, but it is sin living in me that does it. So, I find this law at work: Although I want to do good, evil is right there with me. For in my inner being I delight in God's law; but I see another law at work within me waging war against the law of my mind and making me a prisoner of the law of sin at work within me." Romans 7:15-23

I read those verses over and over until I felt like I understood them. I didn't open this book to hear any kind of word from God. I didn't seek to understand or be changed by it. I was merely filling the empty space of my mind with words on a page. But something was slightly shifting within me as I read. It wasn't only the way I was thinking, but also the way I was feeling.

I didn't know if this moment could be considered a spiritual revelation, or if somehow God was speaking to me through the words I was reading, but I decided right there and then that I was going to do the opposite of what I'd been doing so far. I was going to plead guilty and take the deal at my next court date. I knew that prison would change me forever and, for a moment, I considered how it might change me for the better. I started to see a light and a hope in the last place I ever imagined I would find it.

It was settled. I was going to prison.

Once my time in the hole had come to an end, I made my way to my new housing pod and began my mental preparations. I had been incarcerated for more than five months by then, and my next court date was fast approaching. Once a guilty plea is entered, it doesn't take long for sentencing to happen. They ship inmates out on a bus headed for prison pretty quickly after that.

"Hey Regina, can I ask you something?" I said to one of my fellow pod-mates one afternoon.

Regina had been in the county jail for well over a year, fighting a case that would be her third strike. If she fought and lost, she'd be facing far more time than the two years I was looking at. She had spent much of her adult life in the California State penitentiaries and knew the ins and outs of the system far better than any lawyer or officer you could find.

"Yeah, girl, what's up?" she asked, rubbing her hand over her shaved head and walking closer to where I sat.

"I'm thinking about taking the deal that the DA is offering. Two years, double credit for the time I've already been here. It would be my first time going upstate. You think I should go or keep fighting?"

"Ah girl, you should just do the time. Parole is way better than all those probations you got now. The commissary is better. And there's yard time daily, not this one hour on the roof every three weeks that we get here." she replied.

"Okay, but what about after I get out? If I'm gone that long, I might not be able to find a place to stay after that."

"They help you find a spot to release to, a halfway house or sober living. And all those fines you got right now—wiped out. They don't charge you anymore, you just gotta pay your parole fees. Just take the deal. I could do fifteen months standing on my head."

"Yeah, you're probably right," I said. I ended the conversation feeling even more confident about my decision.

On the morning of what was to be my final court appearance, I made the long walk down the blue corridor with mixed emotions. I felt peace that I would finally have an outcome, but I also felt anxious to enter a guilty plea. I sat in the brown holding cell until my name was called, then walked out to the cage to await the conversation with my public defender on the other side of the chain link fence.

"Harris, nice to see you again." She continued before I had a chance to respond.

"The DA has decided to extend you one last option for a deal. If you sign today with an admission of guilt for the trafficking charge, they'll drop everything else and enter you into a joint suspension for two years. By signing the agreement, you promise to stay out of jail, abide by the law, and complete all requirements of your probation for three years. Then you'll be entered into what they call an extended sentence. You'd be released by tomorrow morning."

I was stunned. Out by the morning? I had just gotten comfortable with the idea of prison, and now I'd be out by morning? I responded to her with the only thing I could think of to say. "What happens if I can't stay out of jail for two years?"

For the past four years, I hadn't been able to stay out of jail for more than a few months at a time, sometimes less. I instantly doubted my ability to honor any agreement I made.

"If you are arrested for anything in the next two years, you will auto-matically receive a two-year prison sentence without a new trial, on top of any sentence you receive for any new charges you may collect."

Even with that answer, all I heard was "out by tomorrow" so I agreed to the deal. The judge agreed to the deal too, and within an hour I was signing a document promising to stay out of trouble for the next two years with very little hope that I'd actually be able to stick to it.

The next morning, I heard the most beautiful words an inmate can hear right before breakfast.

"Harris, roll it up."

I'd already had my belongings rolled up and ready to go, and as the cell door clanged open, I made my way through to each section of the jail towards the door that led to freedom. I could see girls looking out the glass windows at me, with expressions that said they were wishing we could magically trade places. It was the same way I had looked at other ladies at the moment of their release pretty much daily since my arrival. I changed out of my county blues and into my street clothes that fit quite a bit more snugly than I remembered. And I felt the sweet release of my arm band being cut off by the deputy as I walked out the final door.

I was finally free. Or so I thought.

REFLECT

Desperation comes in many forms. The longer I went without sleep, the more boundaries I was willing to cross and rules I was willing to break for just a little rest. Having no escape from my current reality felt suffocating, and being forced to experience this reality clean and sober while also being unable to sleep through any portion of it felt like a slow torture.

Maybe you have experienced a similar level of desperation. A deep desire for something to be different in your life. Perhaps you have wished, and prayed, and longed for something so deeply that the lengths you were willing to go to reach the desired outcome included crossing boundaries or breaking rules, doing anything to find an ounce of peace or get the result you most wanted.

The same was true when it came to my release. I knew right away how dangerous it was to sign an agreement promising to stay out of trouble, but the sheer desperation for freedom overpowered anything I knew. I was willing to take whatever steps necessary to have even a taste of it again.

There is a peace that accompanies taking responsibility for our actions. Even when the consequences are not what we want, and we know we may have to face something difficult, owning up to what we may have done takes us out of a victim mentality and allows us to step into whatever comes next. Whether it was a prison sentence or a contracted promise, admitting my guilt removed a heaviness that had been weighing on me since the day I read those Bible verses.

We all chase freedom. Whether we feel trapped in a broken relationship, trapped in a career we hate for the larger portion of our lives, trapped in a body we don't love or a mind we can't quiet, that sweet desperation to escape our circumstances is vivid and powerful. Sometimes, we are willing to do anything to just feel like we are free. Desperation in and of itself is not a bad thing, it only becomes bad when we allow that desperation to lead us into dangerous places we would usually never go. It becomes destructive when we are facing danger and ignore it for any chance at getting something we want. The line must be drawn somewhere.

REFLECTIVE QUESTIONS

1. Stories have the power to shape how we think and what we believe. Is there a story you've read or heard that changed your perspective on a certain topic? What changed for you and why?

_____

_____

_____

_____

2. Freedom is more than a simple thought or feeling, sometimes it can be what guides you toward your best life. What does true freedom mean to you? How different would your life look if you lived in that freedom?

_____

_____

_____

_____

3. Desperation is often described as a loss of hope that drives people to take reckless action. What are you most desperate for? What lines might you be willing to cross to get what you want?

_____

_____

_____

_____

Chapter 4
Walking Backwards

"No man ever steps in the same river twice,
for it's not the same river and he's not the same man."

~ Heraclitus

I was out of jail, but I had absolutely nothing and nowhere to go.

My routine upon release had always been the same. I would walk across the street to the gas station, spend the only $5 I had saved on my books on a pack of cigarettes and a soda, and walk from there to the neighborhood nearby where I knew a few people.

This time was a little different. First of all, I didn't have $5 on my books. I'd been in jail for so long, with back-to-back arrests, and I'd expected to go to prison, so I had already spent what little money I did have. Second, no one lived in the houses around the block anymore. There used to be a shady bail bondsman in the neighborhood who was always hanging around the criminals he'd helped bail out, trading favors to feed his drug habit. But after they raided him, everyone I knew disappeared, and the houses were left empty.

My cell phone was dead, and there was no charger in my property, so I couldn't call anyone. Not that there would have been any service on the phone even if I'd been able to charge it. I hadn't spoken to a soul since my arrest other than those who'd made it into the same pod as me and could provide an update on the streets, but it had been a while since that had happened. I had no idea where to go and no way to get there.

So, I started walking.

There are many things about being released from jail that prove to be harder than the time we spend in it. No one who's been there routinely likes to talk about that part, because we're all so happy to not be treated like a puppy at a pound anymore. But society and our own jaded life choices have a way of keeping criminals stuck in a life of crime.

There's an emptiness that covers some of us once we realize that no one really missed us while we were gone. That the world was still spinning, the days were still passing—time didn't stand still for them like it did for us. That we won't be able to suddenly have a home, a car, a job, or a family just because we aren't sleeping in a cell anymore. The opportunities for people like us to really try and get our lives together... there aren't many. It takes hard work and support. It takes people willing to offer a helping hand to someone else who has no way to repay them. And right then, I had none of that. I had a history of backsliding, trying and failing again and again, and a reputation for leaving the programs and places that offered help in a fleeting moment of pride and hostility. By this point, no one would have wanted to help me even if I'd asked.

What choice did that leave someone like me? I had been a homeless couch-surfer for five years. I hadn't been able to hold a job since I was working retail during my last stint at rehab a few years prior, and even with that job, I had been escorted out in handcuffs. Security thought I had stolen and spent a gift card from behind the counter.

While that may sound like one of the smaller crimes I'd ever committed, I really was innocent of the accusation. I mean, I did it, but I'd replaced the cost of the gift card with money from my wallet. Who knew that was a crime? But, being a felon already on multiple probations, no one would have believed me anyway. So I let them fire me without a fight, and they agreed not to press charges.

I had burned plenty of bridges. I had lost plenty of friends, either to death, or to the prison system, or to my own twisted understanding of what friendship was. I had pushed my family so far away that I could never call on them for help. I had severely damaged the integrity of my name and my reputation. I had pieces of my life scattered all around me on the floor, and picking them up by myself seemed like a daunting task. I knew nothing other than what I had always known and so, once again, that's what I looked for. Familiarity.

So, I walked. I walked more than eight miles to the track, which marked a small neighborhood I frequented, to the house where I was staying before my arrest. I walked right back to the same life, the same people, and the same behaviors. Because that's all I had.

I knocked on the door. My friend Darren answered it quickly and seemed genuinely happy to see me, which was a welcome change from how most people answered the doors in my life.

Darren had always been kind to me. He was a rocker and music lover at heart who wore his hair in long dreads that fell down his back and almost always had a guitar close by. He preferred pot to the harder drugs but would partake if it came in the house. He was gentle and kind, and one of the few people I knew who treated me like a human no matter what.

I had started crashing at Darren's house off and on about a year before my most recent arrest. He would give up his bedroom and sleep on the couch, offering me privacy and space. He was the closest thing to a family I'd had in a while, and we'd often refer to each other as brother and sister.

When he first took me in, I was an avid hustler. I brought in money, dope, and whatever else we'd need or want. The hustle often came with a lot of movement that would all land on his doorstep. Addicts, dealers, fiends, skinheads, gangsters—you name it. He didn't seem to mind the activity, and we all liked and respected him enough to not let the chaos destroy his home. This lifestyle wasn't without its challenges, but we always figured them out the best we could.

In between my last jail visit and this most recent one, I had taken a turn and fallen down a spiral that was hard to break. I called my mom after my release from the back bedroom of a random drug house. She told me bluntly that my son's father had died in a tragic accident while I was in jail. I was shocked and heartbroken on a level that I couldn't have expected. I broke down right there in some of the deepest sobs I'd let out in a long time, and which I would not let out again for many years.

My son's father was an enigma—a tortured soul who would give you the shirt off his back just as quickly as he'd take yours. He was strong and conflicted and had had a hard life from birth, with an abusive father who was often incarcerated and an addict mother who never seemed to get it together. We met when I was sixteen and he was twenty-three, which sounds crazy when I look back on it at the age I am now. It never seemed that crazy back then in Las Vegas, where rules about age paled in comparison to the other illegal activities that were taking place. I never felt like I was much younger than he was, having left behind childlike behaviors so I could fit in with those around me a long time before. The day we met, he walked into the party pad I frequented and stuck a spit-soaked finger straight into my ear. The tough guy introduced himself to me as Mike with a wet willy… and I fell madly in love with him.

Unfortunately, he was much older and in a long-term relationship with his high school sweetheart. So we spent most of our time together as friends wrapped up in chaos and insanity that varied from one day to the next. I lived a similar life to him as far as drugs and other daily habits, but as a young girl, I would find myself in situations that I needed to be rescued from a lot. He was an excellent rescuer.

As a small child, Mike had tragically lost his baby brother to pneumonia after trying and failing to get him to the hospital on time by himself. He seemed to carry with him this belief that if he'd only been stronger, or smarter, or faster, he would have been able to save him. Rescuing me from myself and those who would seek to harm me became a temporary reprieve from the guilt he felt for not being able to rescue his brother.

I was reckless and often lacked common sense. We can blame that on age or a disregard for my own sanity or safety, but I made choices that would land me in precarious situations on many occasions. I would leave the party house with random guys and need to be picked up from shady motels the next day, share drugs with strangers that could have been cut with literally anything, and commit low-level crimes with shady characters who couldn't hide the proclivities that made them suspicious. Somehow Mike always knew where I was when I would send a 911 emergency message to his beeper. He would show up immediately every time. As I grew more certain that he would always be there to save me, I made even riskier decisions and believed I was untouchable in some ways. That didn't always prove to be true, but I felt a greater bravado each time he showed up when I called.

Mike was respected and powerful, well known and feared. He had *Blue Eyed Devil* emblazoned on his back in deep black ink, and he walked with confidence and certainty. Those blue eyes seemed to soften him if you looked deeply enough, and they disguised the boldness he actually possessed. Inside his eyes, I always saw a broken boy who didn't know where his place was in this world and would seek it out in violent and destructive ways.

The people we surrounded ourselves with had that same double-minded way of thinking. In some ways, we were loyal to a fault and in others, everyone was fair game if we wanted something badly enough. We would find humor in patronizing certain people or playing mind games with others, and we all lived based on a law that we'd created for ourselves. We had our own set of moral codes.

LJ was small in stature but full of charm. His smile made the girls melt and he always seemed to speak to each one like she was the only person in the world. He would drive over to the high school in fancy cars and give us just enough dope to keep us hooked. But he'd only let certain ones join him on his daily adventures. I was in that group for a while and was quickly accepted at the party pad.

Most of the other girls had to find their own way to get to him after a while. Some of these girls couldn't handle their high, and we'd find them locked in the bathroom for hours digging imaginary bugs out of their skin. Others would attach themselves to any one of the available men and be passed around from one partner to the next just to be able to maintain her spot in the house.

Rico was in the country illegally but was our main drug connect. He ran his business from the back bedroom of a rundown trailer with a steady stream of customers coming and going all day. Now and then he'd get deported, but he was never gone for long. He'd show up again, carrying a bigger bag of meth than when he left, ready to pick up right where he'd left off.

Brett brought the guns. He would sit at the table with a mini arsenal, letting the whole crew participate in the taking apart, cleaning and putting back together of each one. His baby face was disarming, creating the illusion that he could never be capable of causing any harm. But he and his friends were more dangerous than they seemed.

Dre wasn't just a meth user, he also smoked crack. We could always tell when he had mixed the two. His whole demeanor would shift. He could sometimes be seen twisting a razor blade around in his mouth, thick drops of blood pooling at the corners of his lips. He was vocal about his preference for younger women and would develop sick fixations on girls half his age. He'd sometimes carve their names into his calf with that same razor blade and turn vicious when his advances were rejected.

Tragedy and anarchy mixed among the loud rap music and late-night banter. Walls were covered in graffiti art and tagged street names. These men were both the greatest friends I've ever had and the scariest men I've ever known, and I found myself becoming more like them all the time. The delicateness of being a young girl was overtaken by my new harsh and violent persona, where I felt more valuable the meaner I became and the less I regarded others and society as a whole as important.

Though Mike and I were always close, the romantic feelings I had for him were one-sided for a long time. But eventually, that changed. It became an affair. I was a secret to his girlfriend, but not really to anyone else, and he had all but stamped his name on my forehead so no other guys would show much interest in me. It didn't matter to me. I would have followed that man to the ends of the earth—and in some ways, I did.

When he and his sweetheart finally broke it off, I thought for sure I'd be able to emerge from the shadows and have a real relationship with him. But instead, he got into another one. I could never understand why I wasn't good enough, pretty enough, or smart enough for him to just *choose me*, but I was so in love and so used to my secret infatuation that I went along with him anyway for years. Other guys would come and go for brief specks of time, but I always ended up back with Mike.

When I got pregnant at barely nineteen years old, he was twenty-six, and his current girlfriend was pregnant as well. She was much further along. On top of that, he'd been fighting a case for a while and was likely to start a prison sentence soon. He was already in the county jail the day I decided to tell him I was pregnant with his baby.

To my surprise, his stepfather was there, about to leave the visiting area. He came to tell Mike that his son was born that morning.

"Hey Kels, did you see my stepdad out there? Kinda crazy right? I'm a dad," he said through the buzzing visiting room phone.

"Yeah, I did. Congratulations. I actually came here to tell you something pretty important too," I replied.

"Oh yeah?"

"I actually came... to tell you that... I'm ...pregnant."

"You're what?"

"I'm pregnant," I said.

"Kelsey. You can't be pregnant. I can't have a baby with you. She had the baby this morning. You know she won't even let me see my son if she knows I got you pregnant at the same time. And what about–" he continued until I interrupted.

"I don't know what that has to do with me, Mike."

"What it has to do with *you*? You really wanna have a baby with me? While I'm in prison? You want a kid that ends up just like us?" he asked, his energy elevating.

"I don't know what I want. I just wanted to tell you."

"Well I don't want this. You can't do this. What would you even tell a kid when they grow up and ask about their dad? That he was some convict who couldn't get his life together?"

I didn't know what to say, and I could feel myself beginning to fall apart. I finally stood up from my plastic chair and held up a hand to stop him from continuing.

"I will let you know what I decide to do," I said, hanging up the phone and walking away. I fell down outside the facility doors in tears.

Once I had decided to keep our son, I wrote him a letter in prison. I poured out the way I felt about him and how I believed I could see the person he so often tried to bury. I could see the man that he wanted to be in flashes and glimpses all the time, and I knew that a good man lived somewhere inside of him.

That is who I will tell our child about. The man I have always believed you could be, and not the man you are, I wrote.

Nine months after my baby was born, he was released. By then, my mother had decided to move us to California. After an unfortunate run-in with the police at our home, we realized that my criminal connections in Las Vegas didn't make for the safest environment to raise a baby. It was time for a new start.

Then Mike called on the phone and said he wanted to meet his son. I was elated and stayed behind with the baby for a few days as we set a date for him to come over. But he never showed. So, I loaded up the car and my son, Carter, and we drove five hours through the desert from Las Vegas to California.

I'd heard stories over the years about what he was up to—none of it good—but we never spoke again. That jail visit was the last time I saw his face.

Now, it was almost seven years later. He was in a car with a girl, and the police were attempting to pull him over for warrants. But instead of stopping, he ran and initiated a high-speed pursuit. The chase ended with him wrecking and the car exploding. Both he and the girl died in the fiery crash. A tragic end to a tragic life.

The news of his passing hit me so hard that my mother was actually surprised. She said she didn't think I'd get so upset after being apart for so many years. In some ways, it surprised me too, that my hard heart could still feel pain to this caliber, but this death was bigger than many of the other deaths I'd experienced. This was my first love, the father of my child, and the only man I had ever fully trusted and shared the secrets of my life with. I couldn't imagine living in a world where he no longer existed.

My sporadic sleep became interrupted by nightmares where I was in the car with him instead, our son strapped into the backseat. In this reoccurring dream, only our son would survive and he would be comforted by officers telling him that losing his parents was probably the best thing for him. *They were bad people. The world is better off without them*, the dream officer would say.

I spiraled hard and fast into a dark place after this. I was desperate to numb the pain, and the regular amphetamines wouldn't cut it anymore. I needed something stronger.

I fell into a whole new world of addiction, smoking and snorting heroin daily. It wasn't the first time I had dabbled in opiates—using them occasionally to counteract the upheaval of stimulants—but this time was different. This time I had let it take me into the darkness, into the nod and the euphoria of emptiness.

Darren watched this progression firsthand, and how I went from movement and hustle to wasted time and excess sleep. I was sick when I had it and sick when I didn't. I would use meth and heroin at the same time, and neither would achieve the desired result.

As the addiction to heroin increased, the types of people I would need to be around to maintain a high shifted. My line of morality, of even street morality, was easily crossed. No one was my friend, no one was safe, nothing was off limits. I only wanted to stay in the dark, regardless of what it cost me. I took risks that I knew were outrageous, and I stole from both people I cared about and people I feared. I had strangers approach me with information about hits that were out on me all the way from shotcallers in prison, because I'd burned someone they were affiliated with. I didn't care. The depth of this pain evaporated any semblance of a life worth living anymore.

Sure, it seems like an extreme reaction in retrospect, but I already felt like I had so little to live for as it was. Deep inside me, I had still carried the hope of reconnecting with my one true love and our son to be a real family someday. Now, that was completely off the table. I couldn't find the point to anything anymore.

That was how I left things with Darren. Now, almost six months later, he stood at the door with a smile. He didn't hesitate when he asked me if I was done with the heroin before letting me in.

"You weren't the same on that stuff. I love you, and you're always my sister, I just can't stand seeing you like that," he said with a sigh.

"Yeah... I don't know how I let it get so bad. I don't have coping skills or something. But that's the past now... so what did I miss? Can I come in?"

"Well, you've been gone a while this time. My dad ended up moving back in. We can hang out in the garage for a bit, but you can't stay here anymore. Sorry, sis."

"Oh, that's okay. I'll figure something out. Who else is around here?"

He named all the people that lived in the neighborhood and gave me an update on each of them. I can't say I was very interested in the news, unless it helped me figure out who would let me crash at their house for a while, so I didn't have to stay on the streets.

Luckily, Darren had held on to all my stuff while I was incarcerated. Usually, I would get released and it would have all been pilfered, stolen, or lost. Once, a chick who apparently really didn't like me very much burned everything I owned in a backyard. So, two to three times a year, I would start over completely, collecting new things from random people or from stores with weak security teams. I was so desperate to find something to wear after I got out of jail once that I went to the mall to steal an outfit and was caught. I was taken back to jail within twenty-four hours of my release because I couldn't find any clean clothes.

I ended up walking over to a friend's house that had let me crash in the past. She lived right down the block from Darren, and I had stayed with her sporadically over the years for a few days at a time. I caught her right as she was leaving and she let me in. She said she would be out visiting her kids for a few days, but that I could stay until she got back.

Now that I'd been clean for six months, I replayed some of my life decisions while I was locked up and truly understood that I was potentially in a lot of trouble with a lot of people. I mostly wanted to stick to myself for a day or two to get my bearings. But no sooner had I closed the front door then I heard a knock and someone calling my name from outside. Within an hour of opening that door, I had a meth pipe back in my hand.

REFLECT

When pain touches the deepest parts of who we are, it's only human to want to make it stop by any means necessary. But the things we turn to for relief—distractions, substances, habits—often don't heal the hurt; they just bury it. The more we avoid, the further down those emotions go, until we find ourselves wrapped in a comfortable numbness. And when the pain feels too vast, too endless, or too big, the urge to cling to that numbness can become overwhelming. We reach for more, and then more again, chasing relief that never truly comes. We chase that relief to our own detriment.

Insanity has been described as repeating the same thing over and over again and expecting a different result. The concept of being trapped in a cycle and habitually finding myself in the same mess was a tale as old as time for me. I didn't know how to break the cycle, nor did I believe that I ever would. The insanity was my entire life, not a piece of it that I could break free from. Everything would need to change to stop the insanity.

Who do we blame when it comes to these cycles of behavior? Are we entirely at fault? Or are we sometimes victims of a broken system that's been designed to keep us in this spiral of repeated mistakes and behaviors? Do we lack the skills to change, or the resources? Is addiction only a dependency on a chemical or are there pieces of it that stem from isolation and an inability to find connection and support?

We use so many different vices to numb the pain we feel deep down inside. Whether we turn to drugs or alcohol, shopping, sex, food, even exercise… finding a band-aid to cover the wound only works for so long. Eventually, the pus from the injury starts to seep out the sides of the latex sheet, and we can't continue denying its presence anymore. We have to nurse the wound.

REFLECTIVE QUESTIONS

1. Cycles of abuse, pain, or hardship can keep us from growing into our best selves. Have you ever felt stuck in a cycle like this? If so, what was it?

   _____

   _____

   _____

   _____

2. Numbing painful emotions can feel easier than facing them, but it often causes more harm than good in the long run. What have you turned to in order to numb yourself? Did it help you heal, or is the wound still there?

   _____

   _____

   _____

   _____

3. "The road to hell is paved with good intentions." What does that saying mean to you? Can you think of a time when your intentions were good but the outcome didn't go as planned? What happened?

   _____

   _____

   _____

   _____

Chapter 5
Thriving in Chaos

"Chaos was the law of nature.
Order was the dream of man."

~ Henry Adams

Not even three days passed after my release before I had a run in with the police. I stood in the driveway of a house around the corner from where I'd been staying while the cops looked for one of the guys inside. They pulled us all out one by one and slapped the shiny silver cuffs on our wrists, and I thought for a moment about how ridiculous it was that I could so quickly find myself in this same scenario yet again.

This was a small beach city in Southern California. Most of us undesirables were well known by the officers, and vice versa. I mostly treated them with respect, but I knew I'd flown a little too close to the sun with that department on multiple occasions, so the way they chose to treat me on any given day was always a surprise. I'd had experiences that ranged from perverted stalker cop, to downright mean cop, to tiny lady cop trying to prove herself tougher than her five-foot-two stature would have you believe. But it would be unfair to not mention the officers who would give me pep talks, free passes to try and give me a leg up, or life advice that they thought I needed. In my experience, the dichotomy of law enforcement is just like what you've probably seen on police television shows a dozen times.

As I stood in that driveway, my heart pounded. The officer walked me through the narcotic sobriety test. Close your eyes, tilt your head back and count to one hundred. Follow the pen light with your eyes—left to right and then left again. To me it was obvious that I was a walking 11550 (the code for being under the influence of a controlled substance) but they weren't there for me. They finished what they came to do and left, after taking the cuffs off my wrists. I released the loud sigh of relief that had been built up in my chest for the entire duration of their visit.

Something about that moment struck me as I walked away from the house while the police drove away behind me. That two-year prison sentence was inevitable. There was no way out of it, and all I was doing at this point was buying myself time. What happens if the next run-in results in a new arrest with new charges and my time doubles?

By this point, prison didn't sound as good to me as it had while I was already sitting in a cell, so I knew that I had to get out of that town. I needed someplace where cops didn't know me quite as well, so I could fly under the radar a little while longer. The plan came to me in an instant.

I had gone back and forth from Las Vegas a few times over the years when things would get too hard in the town I was in. Most of the time, I would drive to and from in a stolen car, coming back just in time for the check-ins with my probation officer and to visit with my son. Vegas was bigger, so it was easier to stay hidden, and I wasn't dealing with every officer in town knowing my face and pulling me over to see what they could catch me for this time.

I called my Vegas bestie, Shannon, and we made a plan. If I could get to the state line between Nevada and California, our friend Mack would meet me and bring me back to her house. I wasn't sure yet how I would get to the state line, but I agreed and told her I'd keep her updated. I knew, sooner or later, I would get caught in Vegas too, but at that point, they would have to extradite me back to California anyway, which would potentially buy me more time in county jails and less time in prison. I know it doesn't sound like the greatest idea, but at the time, it was the best I could come up with.

So, one more time, I made a plan to go to prison. This time, though, I planned to take the long way.

I knew that my other friend, Anna, had moved in with her dad in Los Angeles County before I got busted. I assumed she was clean, probably had access to a car and some gas money, and would maybe be willing to pick me up and drive me to the state line to meet my friend. So, I gave her a call that same day. By the next morning, she was in the driveway helping me load my bags into the trunk of her car.

Except, Anna wasn't clean. And she wasn't staying at her dad's. Instead, she drove us almost two hours away to a beach house that looked gorgeous on the outside, but like every other drug dump I'd ever been in on the inside. The guys who lived there were wild, and it showed in their home. The doors were broken at every entrance, the couch had burn-marks covering the fabric, the kitchen cabinets hung off the hinges, revealing the few canned goods that were available for them, even though they didn't eat much because they were too high. After being there for only a few hours, I figured out just how wild they were, because they chose injection by needle as their primary form of drug ingestion.

Meth creates chaos no matter how you do it, but those who choose this intravenous route expose themselves to an instant rush of amphetamine. The direct hit to the bloodstream seems to ignite aggression and even some delusion, definite over-exhilaration, and peaked volatility.

This level of reaction lasts about thirty minutes, but the high itself can go on for as long as twelve hours, sometimes even longer, depending on how much you take. You can still function to an extent, but hiding the fact that you're under the influence is pretty hard to do with jerky movements and uncontrollable behaviors that give you away.

Thank God, I hadn't ever chosen that route, even though I'd had plenty of opportunities to do so, and my tolerance level had all but maxed out with smoking and sniffing. I just couldn't do it. I would always think of the guy I met at a tweaker pad when I was fifteen years old and still relatively innocent to the severity of the drug world.

It was summer in Las Vegas, when the temperatures reached 110 degrees on most days. A guy had shown up to pick up some dope from my friends. He wore a black leather jacket and a long-sleeved flannel shirt. He was covered in sweat and kept grabbing at the crook of his arm and flinching. After he scored, he asked if he could "hit up" there before he made his way to the hospital to have his arm checked out. I heard the dealer say yes from the other room.

I didn't know what "hit up" even meant. About fifteen minutes later I walked into the room where he was getting high.

The guy had his sleeve rolled up above the elbow and was anxiously trying to stab something I had never seen before into his arm. It looked small and sharp, and I slowly recognized it as a small, hypodermic needle, though I'd only ever seen one in pictures during D.A.R.E class in fifth grade, or when I was taken to the doctor for shots as a kid. Upon closer inspection, I saw that there was a deep, red-black hole in the inner part of his elbow—an obvious infection that seemed to permeate around the pointed edge of the needle that had blackened the skin. It surprised and disgusted me.

Later, I heard that the guy lost half his arm to gangrene. And he still came back for more dope.

There was no way I was going to last in this house for very long, and luckily, I didn't have to. Some other guys showed up later that evening to collect some money. At first the tensions were low, and there was banter and humor amongst the two groups. But suddenly, total anarchy broke out in the living room of what would now be a million-dollar beach house in Marina Del Rey.

Arguments erupted, punches were thrown, and as the sounds of loud crashes and shouts began to carry to the neighbors, Anna and I snuck out the front door, trying to escape before the cops ended up there too. I was sure I didn't have warrants yet. I had only been out for a few days, and there was a thirty-day timeframe to check in with probation. But there was still no way that I'd slide through another arrest that quickly after the last police encounter.

After leaving there, we did end up going to Anna's dad's house. We drove about twenty more minutes up the Marina Expressway. Her dad was an older man who seemed to live a quiet life and would do what he could to take care of his adult daughter, despite her addictions and the turmoil he'd undoubtedly endured from them. I couldn't tell if he really believed she wasn't using, or if he kept the proverbial blinders on over his eyes to avoid having to actually confront the issue. My mom was the same way for many years.

We stayed there for a few days, but we'd leave during the day to get high or find some kind of meaningless trouble we could get into in the area. As the days continued to pass, there was very little mention of taking me to the state line, despite my requests and reminders that it was the whole reason I was there in the first place.

She was eager to introduce me to new people in her hometown. The introductions ranged from random men who had befriended her, to neighbors she'd known for years, to a high-profile lady drug dealer who ended up taking a liking to me and wanting me to join her on her escapades. I left all but one duffel bag at Anna's house and went with the lady drug dealer to spend a few days at hers.

The woman wore her dyed-black hair in a sharp A-line cut, a fitted leather jacket over all-black clothing, and four-inch heeled boots that added a little height to her petite frame. The sharp click of her heels echoed with every step, announcing her arrival to anyone paying attention. At first, all was well. She was laid back and generous, and she kept me from the pain of withdrawal. I was helpful and kept my personal drama to myself.

She didn't bring any sales activity into her home. Instead, she left during the day to make drug runs. The first few days, she brought me with her, and we gallivanted through LA County dropping bags off to a variety of addicts. I had participated in these types of adventures countless times before, but the dealers had primarily been men, so to see a woman with such a high level of power receive so much respect everywhere she went was rare and exciting. Eventually, she asked if I'd stay at her house and do some cleaning, specifying certain areas that were off limits. She was so busy building her drug empire that her house was in shambles and needed some attention. She left me with a small bag of meth, and I started cleaning.

When she got back and inspected the areas I'd worked on, she saw a table that I had cleaned and flew into a total frenzy. I was caught entirely off guard.

"What did you do, scrape this table for scraps?! I left you with plenty of dope!" she shouted.

"I didn't even realize that was dope, I just cleaned the table," I responded calmly.

"Oh, now you're lying to me. I bet you used a credit card and scraped residue straight into your pipe. Oh wait, aren't you a bum? You probably don't even have a credit card!" She stomped around her kitchen, with the click, click, click of her heels elevating an already chaotic rant.

Ordinarily, someone talking to me with such hostility would have resulted in a physical altercation, as I'd never been all that great at keeping my temper contained. But in this scenario, I understood my position. I was very much on my own in an area where I only knew one other person, and I had no idea where Anna was. So, I let the drug dealer yell at me. When she called a couple guys I had never met to pick me up and get me out of her house, I went with them without argument.

The two guys weren't so bad, although at this point, my memory of them is rather vague. One of them offered to take me to his house after I explained that I didn't have anywhere to go until I could reach my friend Anna to come pick me up. He made me oatmeal with peanut butter in it, and we watched *The Price is Right* and continued to get high as we sat on his bed. Eventually, there was a knock at the bedroom door followed by the clicking of heeled boots as the lady drug dealer walked in without waiting for a response.

She was absolutely livid to find me there, as you can imagine. Apparently, this guy was her boyfriend, and she was instantly under the impression that something was going on between us in that room. There was no way I could have known that they were in a relationship, but with a moral compass like mine that always pointed in the wrong direction, I can't say that I really cared either way.

She was still shouting and screaming as the guy pushed her out of the room and closed the door behind him. Once she was gone, he came back asking if I'd been able to reach my friend yet. Anna was on her way.

Once she picked me up, Anna drove us a few more miles to another druggie's house so we'd have somewhere to go for the night. By the time we got there, the adrenaline from all the chaos and excitement from the last several days finally caught up with me, and I was exhausted the moment I sat down. I didn't know how much time had passed since the day we left the track. I wasn't sure when I'd last slept or even rested my eyes outside of my last night in the county jail. After a six-month break from using, then hurdling back into daily drug consumption, my body felt drained and tired. I think I'd been on that couch for maybe half an hour before I fell into a deep sleep, still sitting up.

The next morning, I woke up with itchy eyes—like the itchiest eyes I had ever experienced in my life. They were both red and slightly swollen, and I struggled to see clearly out of either of them. But that didn't stop me from finding the pipe and taking one more hit before figuring out what to do next. By now, Anna had finally agreed to take me to the state line, so I called Shannon to plan where and when to meet in Nevada.

She was crying when she answered the phone. I knew immediately that this couldn't be a good sign, but I was desperate to get out of LA, so I pressed her about sending Mack to come meet me.

"Kelsey, Mack's dead," she said between sniffles. "He was drunk and playing around with his gun last night. He shot himself in the face. He didn't mean to. It was awful. The cops don't believe it was an accident, so they've been cruising the neighborhood all day. I don't think you should come if you're on the run. There's no way you won't get caught."

Wonderful.

REFLECT

From the moment I drove away from the track, time accelerated and chaos ensued. I was no stranger to this. In fact, I've often joked that chaos is the place where I thrive. But the speed at which one bad thing after the next seemed to be happening was enough to make my head spin. I had literally no control over what I experienced or who I encountered, and it felt like I couldn't even pause long enough to evaluate the situation and find a solution. My life was entirely out of my control. Looking back at those days now, I realize how scary this would have been for someone who was in their right mind and able to recognize the danger in front of them.

Even though chaos was what I was used to, somewhere deep inside, I still desired peace. I just didn't know how to find it, and I'm honestly not sure I would have known what to do with it if I had. The first step to stopping the chaos in your mind is to walk away from the chaos happening in the physical world. When things feel entirely out of our control, pausing, stepping away, or finding something different to focus our attention on can slow the progression of the hole we keep digging ourselves into, deeper and deeper.

Control is a funny thing. Do we ever really have it, or is it an illusion to think that we could change the outcome of any given situation? I think it's both. In some ways, we are in total control of our destinies and life choices and in others, things come up against those destinies or choices that we cannot stop or slow down.

We often don't see what is happening to us in the moment. It can sometimes be years before we start to see how intricately we are being pulled into each new life phase. I picture it as a thread—one so small and finely twined that we can't see it with the human eye, but its main job is to lead us through a woven path that was already designed for us. I choose to believe that the thread was designed by a power far greater than we can imagine, to direct us to exactly where we are supposed to be.

REFLECTIVE QUESTIONS

1. Chaos can strip away our sense of control. Describe a time when your life felt consumed by prolonged chaos. How did you respond during that season?

   _____

   _____

   _____

   _____

2. Control is a precarious thing—sometimes we have it and sometimes we don't. How much control do you feel you have over your life right now? How does a lack of control affect your daily choices and experiences?

   _____

   _____

   _____

   _____

3. Looking back on your life, do you recognize something like the thread I described, consistent and guiding, that's been weaving through your experiences? What does it look like, and where do you think it has led you?

   _____

   _____

   _____

   _____

Chapter 6
Reaching the Bottom

"In order to rise from its own ashes, a phoenix first must burn."

- Octavia Butler

By the time my call with Shannon had ended, the old man whose house we were in had answered a knock at the door. On the other side stood the same lady drug dealer who had aggressively pushed me out of her house two days before. Her shadow stretched along the floor in the arch of the doorway as she stood with her hands on her hips, tapping the toe of one of those black heeled boots. She ordered me to leave the house.

While gathering my things to leave, I half-jokingly muttered under my breath about the tracking device I now suspected that she'd hidden in my only duffel bag. I happened to glance toward the couch where I was just sitting, and a dusty birdcage caught my attention. It must have been covered by a blanket the night before, or I'd been too tired to notice it, but there were multiple birds crammed inside. The dirty cage didn't seem big enough to house them all comfortably. It was leaning perfectly against the spot where I'd been sleeping.

We left that house, and Anna drove us a few miles back to the house we had spent the afternoon at the day before. She needed to get home to her dad and couldn't take me with her, so she asked the owners of the house if I could hang out there until she was able to come back to get me. They agreed, but after a few hours, my itchy eyes were bothering me so much that I left. I walked to an Urgent Care that we had driven past a few blocks away. I'd had pink-eye in the past, and I assumed that was what this was, even though it felt way more intense, and I'd never had pink-eye in both eyes at the same time before. Of course, crazier things had happened.

The doctor at the clinic also assumed it was a severe case of pink-eye and prescribed me drops. I procured them from the pharmacy next door and immediately started dripping them in my eyes. But the drops only seemed to make the itching worse. Before the day passed, my eyes were practically swollen shut. I couldn't see anything more than a tiny bit of light through the small slits that I was able to keep open.

I made my way back to Anna's friend's house and stood in the bath-room, borrowing someone's phone to try and find a ride back to the track. I was finally admitting defeat at my attempt to flee to Las Vegas. I called my friend who had always come through for me in the past and told him I was totally blind and stranded, and I had a deranged lady dope dealer kicking me out of every house I walked into.

He laughed, and that made me instantly furious. I didn't find anything funny about my situation, so I started yelling for him to come get me. He listened for a minute, then said he'd send someone my way if I could wait until later that night.

"No, you have to come yourself. I literally can't see anything. I can't stay here. I won't even recognize whoever you send. Just come yourself, please!"

"I can't, Kels. I'm caught up over here. It's him or no one."

"Fine, don't worry about it. I'll figure something else out."

I hung up the phone, knowing that I should have been grateful that he was willing to send someone hours away to pick me up. But I was so anxious that I couldn't find any other emotion to spare but frustration. I walked out of the bathroom and kept to myself.

Time passed without me even realizing it. I have no idea how long I was there, sitting in the corner of a bedroom in a house that belonged to a stranger while I struggled to see and wondered if this lack of sight was some kind of punishment from a higher power. Outside of my little corner, the house was busy. People came and went, using drugs in whatever form they preferred in every room. I was surrounded by people I didn't know and could hardly see while the movement around me carried on without ceasing.

There was a numbness that I let myself drift into. Even with infected eyes and a lack of sight, I still took hits from the pipe when it was offered to me. I still wouldn't allow myself to slow down long enough to try and heal. I needed to stay alert, and while I was aware that the position I was in just kept getting worse, I couldn't even conjure up the thoughts I needed to plan my next steps. The haze of intoxication blurred my ability to think at all.

I knew I needed to go back to Urgent Care because something was definitely wrong, and the eyedrops weren't fixing it. My eyes burned and watered continuously, and there was no way I could keep going like that. After asking someone at the house to give me a ride back to the facility, I went in to see the same doctor I had seen a few days before. I explained to him that I didn't think what I had was pink-eye. After asking me questions about where I had been the night before the itchiness started, he stumbled onto an answer.

He now believed that the infection I had was an allergic reaction to bird dander, a bacteria that lived on their feathers.

I didn't even know that birds had dander, but if there were multiple birds in an unclean cage and my head was next to said cage for multiple hours, it was a likely hypothesis. He gave me a shot in the backside, some new drops for my eyes, and an antibiotic. After waiting there for a few hours, I was able to see well enough to stop panicking that I was about to be blind for the rest of my life.

As I walked back to Anna's friend's house, I knew I needed to call my guy friend back and agree to let his friend come get me. But as I got closer to the house, you'll never believe whose car was in the driveway. None other than the lady drug dealer. Somehow, she managed to be the drug connection for literally everyone in this Culver City neighborhood and somehow, she also just so happened to walk into every house I was in while I was in it. This time, as I walked in, I was just as quickly escorted back out. My duffel bag was tossed onto the ground behind me.

A group of people standing on the lawn called me over. They explained that she never let any of them stay in the house while she was conducting business, and that she'd always been a class-A *you know what*. But she definitely seemed to hate me, because she asked them if I had been there as soon as she walked in the front door and then told them she would cut them off if they let me back in.

As we stood on the lawn, I explained to the group around me what had been happening and how I had no idea what to do next. I poured it all out in desperation to this circle of strangers standing in the grass. One of the girls suggested I walk down to the welfare office and request an emergency shelter hotel room. She said if I lied and said I was pregnant, they'd provide a voucher and a food stamp card right then and there. I was desperate and anxious, and not sure what else to do, so I did exactly what she suggested.

Welfare provided me with a two-week voucher for emergency housing at a motel I'd never heard of, but they wouldn't give me a food stamp card. As backwards as this sounds, because I had a felony on my record for drug sales, I was only eligible for cash assistance, and they couldn't give that to me on an emergency basis. I had to apply for it. But I was happy to take what I could get. I accepted the voucher and left the office with a place to go where I wouldn't be kicked out, dragged away, or left on the lawn.

Up until this point, I had pretty much been operating purely in survival mode. I suppose that's true about my entire life, but it was certainly true about the past few weeks since my release. I struggled to understand how so much had transpired in such a short amount of time and questioned how I had ended up stranded in LA with no way to get anywhere, no money, and no phone so quickly. The only thing I could do now was find my way to this motel, get some rest, and figure out what came next.

I realized pretty quickly that I had no idea where this motel was or how I would get there. I walked around for a while looking for the street name listed on the voucher but had no luck. Feeling defeated, I sat down in front of a donut shop with my duffel bag to catch my breath, staring straight ahead of me but seeing nothing at all.

I'm not sure if this could be described as rock bottom, but it certainly felt like I was deep in a pit of my own construction. I was so on edge, my body felt like it was electrified and buzzing all over. I had zero thoughts happening in my own mind, just an empty slate of nothingness that caused me to stare blankly, not even noticing what was happening around me.

I'm not sure how much time passed while I sat there. I couldn't tell you what was going on or who was walking by. It was like I had gone completely numb and could do nothing but sit and stare.

"Here, would you like this?"

I glanced up toward the voice and saw two young men walking out of the donut shop. One of them held a glazed donut stretched out toward me.

I realized then that I didn't remember having an actual meal since the peanut butter oatmeal, but I declined. I still couldn't see perfectly, and I wasn't sure who these men were. Even if they were safe, I wasn't certain that I wanted to share a breakfast pastry with them in a random parking lot in the middle of my rock bottom. But despite my objection, one of the guys crouched down next to me on the warm concrete.

"My name's Brandon. This is Austin." he said, gesturing to the other guy who was still standing over us. He gave a small wave.

Brandon had dark hair and amber-colored eyes, and he seemed like he might be a few years younger than me. He looked kind and unthreatening. There was a peace around him that seemed tangible and authentic. Austin was a bit shaggier in appearance, with an unkempt beard, a dirty hat with tufts of dark hair sticking out of the bottom edges, and a wife-beater tank top that looked old and stained.

"We saw you out here when we pulled up. Just wanted to make sure you're okay. This is not the best neighborhood for a lady to be sitting around with a suitcase out."

"I'm okay, thanks. I've been looking for this motel, and I couldn't find it. Do you know where this is?" I asked, showing him the address listed on the voucher.

"No, sorry." He started to walk away but paused and turned back around.

"Are you sure you don't want a donut? You can go in and pick out whatever you want, on me." Brandon asked as he stood back up.

"I'm good. Thanks anyway."

Brandon and Austin got back in their car, an old junker by the locks of it, and started to drive away. But before they made it out of the parking lot, I watched them back up as Brandon yelled to me from the driver's side window.

"Why don't you come with us? We can find the motel together. I don't feel right leaving you out here."

I started to decline again, but what else was I going to do? Keep sitting there alone until it was dark? Wait for some weirdo to come snatch my only bag from me, or worse? I gave a slight shrug, then stood up and climbed into the back seat of the old car.

As we started to drive, Brandon started to talk. At first it felt like he was just droning on and on, and all I wanted was for him to be quiet for a few minutes so I could think. But he kept on talking, and eventually I started to tune in to what he was saying.

"Yeah so, after I got out of prison, I went into this sober living home, and I've kind of felt called to help people ever since. I've been clean and sober for three years now. Have you ever thought about getting clean?" I saw him look at me through the rear-view mirror as I felt the surprise wash over my face that it was obvious to him that I was in fact, not clean.

"Um, sure. I've been clean a few times before. I was just clean for six months, but after I got out of jail, I really didn't have anywhere to go so I kinda fell into the same routine, you know?"

"Yep, I get it. I did the same routine for years. This time it's different, though, this time I'm doing it with God. Actually, it was God who told me you needed help. He said I couldn't leave until I helped you."

I couldn't help but chuckle. "Why would God want you to help me? I don't even know him like that."

"Maybe not. But He knows you," he said, with the tone of someone who seemed like he might start preaching at me any second.

"Maybe, but if this is the life He chose for me, I doubt He likes me very much," I said. I turned to look out the window at the upcoming street names. I hoped this shift would convey that I was done with the conversation about God so that we could go back to finding the motel.

We were driving around for a while when suddenly the car started to slow down. A small stream of gray steam could be seen drifting from the front hood.

"Ah crap, we're overheating. We'll have to pull over and let it cool down."

This was obviously not what I wanted to hear and I let out a sigh as he pulled over. As we sat in the parking lot of a dirty gas station in a rather undesirable neighborhood, Brandon started to share his story with me. And since I didn't have anything better to do, I started to listen.

He had been raised in a "kill or be killed" foster care system and had a single mom who was currently residing in a van on the streets of Santa Monica. He'd spent most of his childhood moving around from place to place and never feeling like he had a real home. Of course, this lifestyle isn't easy to maintain, and once he started doing drugs, they became the priority. That priority inevitably led Brandon to his own drug addiction, and to a life of crime. Eventually, he went to prison for two years.

We found that we shared a lot of similarities. We even had the same birthday, although he was three years younger. His story did speak to me, and I felt myself softening to him and what he was trying to do. I ended up sharing a bit of my story too, and he explained that from his experience, trying to get to prison was a bad plan. He kept saying that there was another way to get out of this hole I had dug myself into so deeply. He brought up programs and places that he had learned about since starting on his new quest to help people.

Austin wasn't quite as vocal, but he did say that Brandon was the reason he was clean and at the sober living home. I'm not sure if he'd picked him up off the side of the road like they had me, but it made me a little happy to hear that his journey to help people was gaining traction.

We sat in that parking lot talking for over an hour. I did eventually let Brandon get me something to eat and drink from the gas station, and when he finally decided to try the engine, it started with no issues. After we pulled out of the lot, the very next street was the one we'd been looking for. We had been parked less than a block away from my destination for over an hour—an hour spent in deep discussion about prison, recovery, and God.

Brandon and Austin waited in the car while I checked in at the front desk and carried my solitary bag up to the room assigned to me. They walked me in and stood in the doorway while I plopped down on the bed, exhausted.

"Why don't you get some rest tonight, and I'll come back and get you tomorrow? Take you to get some real food," Brandon said as he walked over to the table and set down some coins for the payphone. He picked up the motel paper and pen and wrote down his phone number. "Call me when you're ready."

After they were gone, I took the coins he'd left on the table over to the vending machine and bought a soda. I poured the soda out and turned the can into a weed pipe, filling it with some dirt weed that I had stashed in a cigarette cellophane wrapper. I smoked the weed with the book of matches I found in the motel drawer and let myself slowly drift off to sleep.

REFLECT

When I think about my three days of almost blindness, I think about the way that Saul became Paul in the book of *Acts*. Saul was set in his ways, committed to the destruction of believers in Christ and traveling down a road set to continue punishing them. He required an extreme experience like losing his sight to be able to see that God was real. It took a step of faith and a walk to a stranger named Ananias for him to receive prayer and have his sight restored.

Now I'm no Saul and definitely no Paul, but perhaps the loss of my sight while on a road leading toward continued self-destruction planted a seed of change in my heart. Then I met a stranger who was willing to show me kindness that I didn't deserve.

Having a stranger step toward me at a time when most people were stepping away reminded me that kindness still existed in the world. Even though Brandon was on a personal journey to reach out to those in need, he could have easily walked right past me. How many people have we walked by without a second glance? How many times have we felt a tug to speak to the man on the side of the road holding a cardboard sign, only to ignore him instead? We never know what kind of change we can make in someone's life in those moments when we choose to stop and really see them.

Hitting rock bottom is different for everyone, and it happens outside of the world of addiction. It can come in the form of ending a broken marriage, losing a loved one, battling an illness, or facing financial challenges. How do we recognize when we've hit our bottom? Are you isolated and alone? Do you feel completely out of solutions with nowhere to go? Have you run out of ideas to get yourself back together, and now you finally feel ready to ask for help? Rock bottom in its simplest form is the realization that things are as low as they could possibly be. We can look at that reality in one of two ways: deciding that everything sucks and now we're stuck on the ground, or recognizing that once we're at the bottom, the only way to go from there is up.

REFLECTIVE QUESTIONS

1. Rock bottom looks different for everyone. Have you ever experienced a rock bottom moment? What did that look like for you and how did you recognize that you were there?

    _____

    _____

    _____

    _____

2. Sometimes we see ourselves as characters from a story, through a shared trait, struggle or experience. Is there a character from a story that you relate to? What about them resonates with you?

    _____

    _____

    _____

    _____

3. Accepting help takes courage, especially when it's from someone we don't know, but we were not created to handle tough situations all alone. Have you ever received help from a stranger? What was that experience like for you?

    _____

    _____

    _____

    _____

Chapter 7
Being Rescued

"Sometimes you can only find Heaven by slowly backing away from Hell."

~ Carrie Fisher

It's probably obvious that I did not call Brandon when I woke up. The sting of coming down off the high I'd been on struck so hard the next morning that my quest to halt the internal skin crawl felt more important than a hot meal. Instead, I went down to the gas station we'd been parked at the day before and begged for change for the payphone.

Once I got enough change for a few calls, I started trying Anna, then one of the guys she'd introduced me to, then anyone else I could think of. No one answered. I slammed the phone down, collected the remaining change, and walked back to the room to try and sleep through the body aches.

The sun was shining brightly into the room when a knock on the door pulled me out of my sleep. I instantly assumed it was a maid, and I yelled that I didn't need anything, but the knocking continued.

I dragged myself out of bed and peeked through the window, seeing Brandon standing there by himself. He gave a slight wave when he saw the curtains move, so I knew I had no choice but to open the door.

"Hey, good morning sunshine. Or should I say afternoon? It's like 3pm, aren't you starving?" The pep in his voice hurt my ears.

As soon as what he'd said registered in my mind, I felt the pangs of hunger erupt in my belly and knew the only way to stave off that feeling would be to go with him. I let him in the room while I went into the bathroom to clean myself up. I felt a little guilty when I thought of him seeing the aluminum can covered in marijuana ash resting on the bedside table.

He took me to the grocery store to buy a few things. After that, instead of taking me back to the motel, he drove to the sober living home where he lived and invited me inside. He said we could cook there since there was obviously no kitchen in the small motel, and I agreed, blindly following along with no real plan or idea of what I should be doing instead. He introduced me around to a few of the guys who lived there, including Marcus, a large black man who appeared to be deep in his studies at the dining room table.

Brandon whispered to me as we walked away from him and into the kitchen, "He's studying to become a pastor." I nodded, but I remember feeling surprised that an addict could ever become a pastor. I thought our lifestyle conflicted way too much, and that once you had reached the stage of needing a sober living home, any potential for becoming a man of faith went out the window.

After we ate, Brandon turned on a movie, and we sat on the couch to watch. I don't think we made it past the opening credits before I was asleep.

That evening, after the movie ended and Brandon had woken me up, Marcus came into the room. He wanted to confirm that Brandon was taking him to church that Sunday and turned and asked me if I'd like to join them.

"What day is it now?" I asked.

"It's Friday. We can pick you up on the way. You'll love it, I promise." Marcus said, with a subtle excitement rumbling in his deep voice.

"Um, yeah, okay. I've never really been to church before."

Church was a mystery to me. In all my life, I had only ever been to a Mormon church once as a child, with my neighbor across the street, and to the outside of another church that served hot meals for the homeless and hungry. Growing up, we also lived next door to twin girls who were Jehovah's Witnesses. They would have some kind of Bible study brought into their homes weekly that I attended once or twice, but as soon as they told me there were no birthdays or holidays, I was out.

There wasn't much conversation surrounding faith in our home. I knew my mother had been raised Catholic and didn't love the things she'd learned in that religion by the time she reached adulthood. My dad would say quippy things like "only God can judge me" and talk about a stairway to heaven and a highway to hell, but there was never any serious discussion about faith or belief systems at any point in my life. We were basically free to explore and decide on our own.

By the time Sunday came around, I was feeling a little better physically and had mostly slept off the residuals of my drug consumption. Brandon had picked me up every day since we met and taken me to the sober living home to hang out. I didn't know it then, but I imagine this was part of his plan to keep me from roaming the mean streets, looking for my next fix. For the moment, it was working.

We pulled into a huge parking lot that was absolutely packed full of cars and walked into a giant, dome-shaped building that in no way resembled a church in my mind. After looking around a bit and seeing cameras and microphones hanging from the ceiling, I guessed this was a televised church service, popular amongst the Black community. It seemed like Brandon, Austin and I were the only white folks in the whole place.

It was overwhelming in some ways, to see so many people truly committed to a faith in something none of them could see, but also one of the coolest experiences I've had. The attendees were dressed to the nines and were obviously excited to be there. The music was incredible, and the man speaking talked about things that resonated with me in ways I hadn't expected. He preached on forgiveness, on finding hope in dark places, on standing firm in faith and not wavering. I began to understand why they televised his teachings, the service, and the music. It felt like I was at a concert.

When we got back to the sober living home, Marcus asked if he could show me a few things. We sat down at the dining room table, and he pulled out his old Bible. The pages were folded and worn, and there were highlighted markings inside over different paragraphs and notes written on the sides. That Bible was the most well-used and well-loved book I'd ever seen.

I can't remember exactly what verses he shared with me that night, but the message was simple. I believed that I was way too far gone to ever be forgiven or welcomed by a God of any understanding. I had lived my entire life so far in a dance with the devil, breaking every one of the commandments and feeling little to no remorse. I didn't believe that I deserved to be saved, rescued, or loved. I was filthy, tarnished, and bad.

And Marcus was telling me over and over that none of that mattered. He said if I surrendered my life, God would forgive me. He said that I was loved. He said that I was precious to Him, and he called me a daughter to a king. He said that no matter how far I had gone in the wrong direction, God could bring me back if I would let him.

The conversation eventually shifted from talk of the Bible to talk of a rehab.

"I know a place. It's less than an hour from here in Santa Monica. We just show up in the morning, and if they have a bed, they take you, first come-first serve, no questions asked. If they don't have a bed, they have an office that will call all the surrounding programs to find one with a space for you," Brandon explained.

"I can't go to a rehab in Santa Monica, I'm on probation a hundred miles away and on a joint suspension," I argued.

"You're already on the run, getting caught in a rehab is better than getting caught on the streets. At least it shows you're trying."

I pushed back with more arguments that consistently fell flat. Brandon had an answer for everything I threw at him—all my doubts and fears. So eventually, I agreed to try.

The next morning, Brandon was at the motel door bright and early to drive me along the 10 freeway to wait in a line that wrapped around the building and see what they would say. It felt strange to stand in a line that led to an unknown outcome, but I wasn't sure what else to do. By that point, I'd been to so many programs over the years that it didn't really matter to me where I ended up anymore.

My first stint in rehab was an outpatient program when I was fifteen. My mom would drop me off twice a week for a group. I think I lasted three weeks before they kicked me out for selling meth to the other kids—which wasn't even really meth, it was all fake, but I had broken the rules, nonetheless. I don't think I had ever stopped using while I was there, anyway.

The next time I tried to get clean was after the death of a friend of mine when we were seventeen. He was a victim of a drug deal gone bad. He'd been stabbed at a park and walked around for a while before lying down and bleeding out on a picnic table. No one around him realized that he was dying right in front of them, as they were too high to notice their own surroundings. After his funeral, everyone sat in a room and smoked their drug of choice. I was disgusted at their behavior. After making that known, loudly and aggressively, I drove home and wrote myself a note that I hung on the wall above my bed.

Today is the day you get to choose something different. You don't have to go back. You don't have to get high. Today is a brand new day.

I got a job at a pre-school as a teaching assistant and went back to a continuation school to get my high school diploma. I did well for a while. But I relapsed about three days before reaching the six-month mark.

The third time I tried to get clean was after my father died, when I was twenty-one years old. Dad had always struggled with addictions of his own, and we hadn't ever really gotten along very well. He had a rage that lived deep inside him that would often result in violence and destruction. He also had another side of him that people always seemed to be drawn to. His humor and laid-back nature pulled you in, but you had to step gently, because he would lose his temper and become the meanest guy you'd ever seen on a dime.

His stories of world travel and celebrity interactions were enticing and exciting, and the way he'd strum on his old guitar and sing about wagon wheels and busted shoes made everyone turn and pay attention. I wonder sometimes if the reason we would butt heads is because we were more alike than we were different, but I never really knew if he loved me or not, and I'm sure the same was true for him. Some days I loved him, and some days I didn't.

These days, when I hear my sisters tell stories of him, I realize that I missed out on ever really getting to know him at all. Whether I was too caught up in my own brokenness or too lost in the idea that he never loved me, I missed the good stuff by always focusing on the bad. That pattern has been true for most of my life.

When I was a teenager, my own addictions started to take over my life, and our fights became more frequent and more hostile. Deep down, I really started to believe that we hated each other. When my parents got divorced and my mother, little sister, and I moved out, we stopped most contact. When I told him I was pregnant at nineteen by a guy he hated, he all but disowned me right then and there. He eventually came around after the baby was born, but the damage had been done, and it was hard for me to forgive and forget all the awful things he'd said and done to me over the years.

Once we moved to California, he slipped back into his own form of using and lost himself in his world while I was lost in mine. He drove out to see us randomly one day and asked me to come back to Las Vegas with him, promising that we could rebuild and come back for my son when I was healthy again. But the breakage of our relationship was too deep, and I declined. I yelled at him about trying to suddenly be a dad when all this time he hadn't bothered and said I'd get clean when I was ready.

A few weeks after that visit, I called him on his birthday. For the first time in a long time, we had a real conversation. He opened up to me about his current addictions and asked me again if I would come back to Las Vegas so we could help each other to get clean. He promised that we could get my son back and create a better life for all three of us. He even cried, and I could count on one hand how many times I had seen the man do that.

This time, I agreed but wasn't really in a place to do so. All I had was a rowdy boyfriend and a stolen car, which my dad agreed I could bring with me as long as I could get there. In some ways, this call was a step toward healing for us—a moment in time where we truly saw each other for who we were: two broken people who never had anyone to teach us how to be anything else.

A few weeks later, on the day that my boyfriend and I had planned to leave for Las Vegas, I waited around for him to show up and ended up falling asleep in the abandoned house we'd been squatting in. No one knew that I was there but him. I'm not sure how long I was asleep, fading in and out as my body recovered from the days of hunger and stimulation, but eventually, a guy I knew found me. He burst through the door with force. The bright sun poured into the room and jarred me awake suddenly, and it took a few seconds for me to focus on who was there and what was happening.

"Kelsey, wake up, girl. We've been looking all over for you. Your mom called. Your dad is dead. You need to get home."

I was so stunned and disoriented that I didn't even catch my breath or fully take in what he'd said. Instead, I asked him to give me a ride to a phone. I called my mom from the living room of a drug house, surrounded by strangers and tweekers, plugging one ear so I could hear what she was saying over the noise they were making.

My dad hadn't shown up for work. My aunt and the police went to his house for a wellness check, and they found that he'd been dead in the house for several days from a drug overdose, surrounded by paraphernalia and evidence of a hard party the night before. A few minutes after I hung up, I was told that the boyfriend I'd been waiting for had fallen asleep at the wheel on his way to come get me, crashed the car, and was arrested for the stolen vehicle. I had been alone and asleep in that house for several days, totally unaware that my whole life was changing outside of it.

I was so desperate to stop the pain I was feeling that I basically vanished, digging myself into a cocoon of isolation where the only people who saw me were the ones bringing me more dope. As the family was grieving together and preparing to head to Las Vegas for the funeral, I was missing. I'd convinced myself that I was to blame for him dying—that I had somehow caused him to over-ingest his drug of choice by not showing up as promised. How dare I show my face at his funeral after being responsible for his death?

But right before it was time to go, a friend found me and talked me into going by saying I would regret it forever if I didn't. I made it to my mom's the night before she and my sisters planned to leave and went with them. Because the decision to go was so rushed, I wasn't able to get any drugs to take with me, and I spent much of the trip in an extreme comedown, missing the family events and final visits to his home because I couldn't pull myself off the floor I was sleeping on.

I spiraled fully out of control after we got back and ventured back out to the streets. I lived with that same lack of coping skills and became a violent and destructive mess, just like my dad. I had no idea how to sit in any type of pain, only drown myself in narcotics until I couldn't even see straight anymore. I had enough self-awareness to recognize that the road I was on was a dead end. I knew if I didn't do something soon, I'd end up exactly where we'd just laid my dad.

I knew of a place down the street from the rundown motel I frequented that helped girls like me. I had seen residents sitting outside on the patio during the day sometimes, having meetings, sipping warm drinks out of mugs, laughing and talking. The allure of what they offered drew me in some days. I wanted so desperately to stop this pain and try something new. Eventually, the desperation to survive finally won.

By the time I hobbled up to the front door of this regular house that had been transformed into an inpatient drug program called the Miracle House, I had bruises all over my face from fights and was on crutches. I had broken my foot when I jumped over a wall running from the police and landed on a parking curb. I knocked on the door and said I needed help, and they let me in.

I learned a lot in that program and genuinely felt like I experienced healing in different ways. But after ninety days inpatient, I was denied access to their sober living home because of my rumored temper. The only option I had was to move back in with my mother and son.

The hard part about this was that my mother had often enabled me—either by trusting me when she shouldn't have or by keeping blinders on to avoid facing the truth about my addiction. Moving back in with her, instead of staying in a structured program, became a bit of a mess, as we often argued about things. I made it maybe three more months at her house, enrolling in college and collecting some student loans, and then being escorted out of the retail job I had for (not) stealing from the register. I couldn't find the point of staying clean if I wasn't welcome around other clean people and couldn't keep a job without landing in handcuffs. I relapsed right before I would have reached six months clean and went right back to the life I knew how to live.

After that, visits to rehab were sporadic, short-lived, or court-ordered. I never lasted longer than a few weeks at a time at any given facility. Sometimes, I didn't even make it for a few days. There weren't many options in the small town where I lived, and I'd exhausted my chances at all of them. I also found that most programs didn't have a lot of awareness about what their residents were doing. Many of the residents weren't even clean. Once rehabilitation became a for-profit business opportunity, rules and regulations relaxed, and patients became necessary whether they were getting better or not. Despite knowing this, I still agreed to give it another go after Brandon talked me into it.

By the time I got to the front of the line to see if there was space for me at this new place, I'd watched them accept a few men and women into the program. I'd watched as others were denied a bed and sent to the building around the corner to start the search for a different facility. When my turn came up, I sat in the seat provided and went through all of the questions with an intake worker, but the one that kept me cut of their program was unexpected.

"Do you receive any financial assistance?" the intake worker asked.

"I'm in a motel on an emergency welfare voucher now and have an application open for General Relief financial aid."

"Ok, what about food stamps?"

"No, they told me I can't have those because of my criminal record."

"Drug sales charge?"

"Transportation, but yeah. I guess that is considered sales," I said, trying to downplay the severity of the situation.

"Unfortunately, because we're a free program, we require you to provide your assistance funds to us. And that, primarily, is a food stamp card. We can't accept the use of your cash General Relief. You'll need to go around the corner to the other office to see if they can find a program that will accept you, but be aware, most places are going to require you to have food stamps. Good luck."

Brandon and I walked out and around the corner with my intake form, and I could feel the weight of discouragement on my chest. But I followed through and sat at the next desk as the clerk picked up the phone and started making calls. Unfortunately, she got the same response from every place she tried. She asked me to come back the next morning at 7am to try again.

We came back the second day and got the same result.

The third day seemed to be following the same course, until she reached what looked to me like the very last name on the list. Finally, we got a yes.

She gave us the information for where to go and a folder with my intake information. Brandon was far more excited than I was. I immediately started to feel anxious and unsure about this decision.

By this point, I'd been clean for about a week, and my mind was in a clear state, so I knew this was the best course of action for my current situation. I still had several bags of belongings at Anna's dad's house that I needed to pick up before being locked away in some building for the next few months. So, I called her from Brandon's phone and planned for him to drop me off with her. We'd collect my items, and she would take me back to the motel in a couple of hours. Brandon would be back for me that afternoon to take me to the program.

"Are you sure about this? We could go grab your stuff right now and go right back to the motel to get the rest and check out. We could have you at the program by dinner time," Brandon said as we pulled up in front of Anna's dad's house.

"I have to gather up all the stuff I have here and try to collect some toiletries and things that I don't have. I'll be fine, don't worry. I'll see you in a couple hours," I said, climbing out of the car. I only had three or four bags of belongings to my name, and while most of it was probably junk that I didn't need, I struggled to lose it for fear I might need it later.

There was a part of me that believed I would be fine—that I could gather my things and be at the motel to meet him in an hour. There was another part of me that had no intention of going to rehab and was desperate to abort the mission and abandon Brandon and this plan entirely. As I walked up the driveway and knocked on the door, I had no idea which plan would win.

REFLECT

In some ways, the decision to listen to Brandon about going to a program was based solely on the knowledge that I had run out of options. It wasn't something I wanted to do. I didn't have a desire to get clean. My only desire was to get off the hamster wheel of life that I'd been stuck on and avoid finding myself in handcuffs again. The difficulty I had in finding a place that would accept me is a reality for a lot of addicts, whether they are desperate to get clean or just going through the motions. Sadly, we don't live in a society that prioritizes helping sick people get well.

Experiencing loss is inevitable in this human life. We don't get to choose when or how someone we love will die or what life will be like without them. Instead, we learn to walk through a new type of pain and learn to navigate a world that they are no longer in. Grieving comes in many forms, and everyone walks through the pain of a heavy loss in their own way. We should give ourselves and each other grace when dealing with grief no matter how many impactful deaths we've lived through.

In instances where we can see clearly that our efforts have been exhausted, sometimes all we can do is seek the advice of another person, preferably someone who has been where we've been and successfully made it to the other side. That's why programs like AA and Al-Anon work. They are based on sharing experiences and teaching the next guy how to get as far as you've gotten.

It's human nature to want to hold on to what we know. Changing lifelong behaviors and habits is like dismantling everything about ourselves and being willing to rebuild from the ground up. It's imperative that we take the time to truly understand why we think and behave the way we do. So many qualities, and defects, that we have in us are rooted in beliefs that we have the ability to change. Changing our beliefs is often the first step in changing our behaviors.

REFLECTIVE QUESTIONS

1. Doing the right thing, even when it's difficult, is a challenge we all face at times. Describe a time that you followed someone else's lead in the opposite direction of where you should have gone. What were the results?

   _____

   _____

   _____

   _____

2. Seeking support during life changes doesn't always lead to the outcomes we hope for. What obstacles have you faced while trying to get the help or support you need?

   _____

   _____

   _____

   _____

3. Faith communities often have varied ways of welcoming newcomers. Describe your first experience with a community of faith. If you've never had one, what stops you?

   _____

   _____

   _____

   _____

Chapter 8
Facing the Music

"Nobody ever did, or ever will, escape the consequences of his choices."

~ Alfred Armand Montapert

I don't remember making the decision or having the conversation, but the next thing I knew, Anna and I were in a garage at some guy's house, and I had a glass meth pipe in my hand. This was a normal everyday activity for me, but for some reason, on this day, the drugs just didn't seem to be creating that same comfortable numbness.

The hours passed by slowly, and I struggled with impeding thoughts. I thought of Brandon showing up at the motel to get me for the drive to rehab and how disappointed he'd be when I never answered the door—so I smoked more.

I started to think of how he and I had driven so far for three days to find a place to go, and now I was blowing it off with little to no thought of what would happen to me when that motel room voucher ran out—so I smoked more.

I thought about Marcus telling me that God would forgive me for what I had done, but instead I'd walked away from that possibility and back to this—so I smoked more.

I thought about my son that I hadn't even seen yet since my release from jail five weeks ago, about the revelation I'd had in the hole at the county jail, about going to prison, about this broken life I was living and the subtle allure of death. It all rolled together into one big ball of chaos inside my mind—so I smoked more.

Sitting in my own reeling thoughts and stifling confusion, I had all but ignored what was going on around me. I had emptied my stress into the glass pipe and inhaled the numbness I so desperately longed for.

Then I looked up.

For the first time in a long time, I saw myself reflected in the people around me. The garage was hot, dirty, and filled with smoke. The people in it were empty of emotion with no life in their eyes. Many of them held needles in their hands. They took each other's arms and tied them off with shoelaces and rubber bands to help with the injection process. There was desperation on their faces as they went to any measure necessary to ingest the methamphetamine poison we were all addicted to. There was a clear ignorance that what we were doing was wrong. I suddenly felt disgusted with myself and them.

I thought about the last few days that I'd spent with Brandon, eating, sleeping, and living normally. I thought about how much I laughed with him and the rest of the guys at the sober living home. Witnessing people who were truly on a quest for something better and were willing to take me along with them was a gift that I was throwing away for this room of nothingness. I thought about how much Brandon had overcome, and what lengths he had gone to to try and help me. And then it dawned on me, in a sudden and unexpected moment of clarity.

I *didn't want* this life anymore!

I *wanted* that one!

It was close to sunrise when I jumped up in a panic and told Anna I needed a phone, and I needed to get back to the motel. I tried to call Brandon, but there was no answer. So Anna had a friend of hers come get me and my bags and take me back to the motel. I tried calling Brandon from the friend's phone, but again, no answer. When I got back to the motel, I took change down to the payphone and started calling again and again with no answer.

I tried all morning to reach him, going back and forth from the motel to the payphone over and over. When he finally answered, I could hear the disappointment in his voice. It took some major groveling and begging for him to agree to come get me and at least see if they would still accept me into the program.

"I messed up, I'm sorry. But I don't want to mess up anymore. I don't want to do this anymore. Please come get me, at least to call and see if they still have a bed."

"Ok fine. I'll be there in twenty," he said with a sigh, and hung up.

The program confirmed that they did still have a space for me, so we made the long drive along the traffic-congested freeway to what looked like a tall corporate building in the middle of the city streets. We took the elevator up to the top floor, and I walked into the hallway with a manilla folder and two duffel bags that I plopped down with a sigh of relief.

The emotions surrounding being dropped off at rehab were the same for me every time. Fear, excitement, anticipation, uncertainty, doubt. The walk in was void of expectation since rehabs often function in uniqueness and not in a uniform way. The standards are similar, but the way each place met those standards varied. Walking into what looked more like an office space than an actual place to live threw me off, but I proceeded anyway.

The staff who greeted us was an older Hispanic woman with an obvious edge. She was classy, but it was evident to me that she was no stranger to the streets. This was the same woman I had spoken to on the phone, and I assumed that she was the program director.

"You must be Kelsey. I'm Sandra. Welcome, I'm glad you were finally able to make it."

"Sorry I'm late. Thank you for letting me come anyway," I said sheepishly.

"I'll give you two a minute to say your goodbyes. You are welcome to write to Kelsey here, we can give you a card with the mailing address at the front desk, but there are no phone privileges for the first thirty days. Is this all your stuff?" she asked, directing her words back and forth from Brandon to me.

"No, there are a couple more bags in the car," I answered

"Okay, well we can get those transferred over to the van, and you can go ahead and take a seat in the case manager's office for your intake process. Are you able to pass a drug test today?"

"No, it would be dirty. Is it still okay for me to stay?"

"Yes, of course you can stay, she said with a small smile. I'm not sure what I would have done had she said anything different.

I thanked her as she stepped away to get a business card from the desk for Brandon. I had just met this guy a week and a half ago, and I still felt like my only friend in the whole world was about to leave me in this unknown place. Between the nerves and the relief, I couldn't form the right words to extend the amount of appreciation that I felt for him in that moment.

"You're gonna be great. Call your probation officer and tell him where you're at. And stay here! Even when it's hard. Promise?" Brandon spoke with a lightness around him, like he thought walking into a rehab miles away from anyone I knew was the easiest task in the world.

I nodded and hugged him, then thanked him and asked him to write. Then I watched him turn and walk back to the elevator, stopping briefly at Sandra's door as she handed him a card with the address on it. She gave him instructions on where to leave my bags. As I watched him walk away, I wondered if I would ever see him again, but I shook the thought off and turned back toward Sandra as she directed me toward another woman's office. The words *case manager* were stamped on the gold plate right outside the door.

The case manager ushered me inside, taking the manilla folder from my hand and gesturing for me to have a seat across from her. We were separated by a desk that was covered in folders and papers.

"Ah Kelsey. We were expecting you yesterday. Glad you finally made it. My name is Melanie, and I'll be your case manager while you're here. Let's get started." She opened the folder that I had gotten two days before.

Melanie was thin and tall. Her wavy hair fell to her shoulders, and her mocha-colored skin shined brightly under the ceiling lights. She picked up a pen to take notes as she started asking me questions about my current and historical lifestyle.

As the conversation progressed, I informed Melanie of my situation with the court—that I was on a joint suspension and hadn't checked in with my probation officer yet. I knew the time allotted to do so was passing by swiftly, but I wasn't really that concerned.

I'd had the same probation officer (PO) for the past four years. Benjamin was young and polite and had always treated me with respect. Even though I usually came to our monthly meetings dirty, with a makeshift way to pass the urine test, he never let on if he knew I was cheating the system or not. He would always recommend the minimum sentence for any violations I collected, which had been quite a few, if we're counting. And he was never super hard on me when I came crawling back for the extension of probation I was repeatedly sentenced to.

"Probation department, this is Ben," he answered the phone.

"Ben, it's Kelsey. I'm sorry I'm a little late to check in. It's been a really crazy month. But I'm in a rehab in LA, inpatient," I said. There was a part of me that hoped his response would indicate that he was proud of me, since I needed affirmation from anyone I could get for making this decision.

"Kelsey! Girl, you're a little late. I tried to wait for you, but I had no choice, I issued warrants for you yesterday," he said.

The irony of this wasn't missed by me. He'd waited an extra week for me to check in before taking it to the courts, which was more than I deserved. And I was now one day late to catching him before he issued the warrants. So basically, if I had come to rehab on the day I was supposed to come and made this call one day earlier, instead of going to that awful garage to get high, I would have made it in time for him to stamp me as compliant on my file.

"Well, what do I do now? Am I going to prison?" I asked, defeated.

"Not necessarily, but you'll have to go to court to clear up the warrants. If you're in a program on self-admission, maybe the judge will give you a chance to finish it before he pulls your extended sentence. But don't wait to take care of this warrant. The longer it ages the worse it looks. You know I'm rooting for you. My recommendation will be to allow you to stay there once it hits my desk. But don't make me regret it, Kels."

"I won't. I'll take care of it. Thanks, Ben."

"You're welcome. Take care." he said and hung up.

I'd been able to keep it cool while I was on the phone, but as soon as the call ended, I felt myself start to panic.

Melanie was very reassuring and explained that there were volunteers who drove residents to places like court and that they would write me a letter for a judge to confirm that I was there at the program. She was much more confident than I was that the judge would accept my current residence and prolong my sentencing. She said things like, "God would not have brought you all this way just to send you to prison," and "Have a little faith."

When Monday came, a woman named Sharon showed up to drive me the hour-plus distance over to the courthouse so I could see a judge and clear my name. The process for clearing warrants was to arrive at the courthouse in the morning and stand in a long line while waiting to talk to a clerk. The clerk would check me in and set me up with a courtroom for the afternoon to get the warrants cleared, if there was space on the docket for any available criminal judge.

Once the courtroom opens, there's more waiting while the judge goes through each case file and calls each defendant to the front. There are no lawyers or public defenders during this part of the process. I would show up, clear my name, and get a new court date.

Sharon acted as a representative of the program, and I turned in a letter confirming that I was currently a resident of an inpatient treatment facility in Los Angeles. By that afternoon, my warrants were cleared, and I had a new date set for thirty days later to review my joint suspension. The judge was very vocal that if I left the program before I came back to court, the odds were that I'd be remanded into custody at that court date.

On the drive back from court, I was able to spend some time talking with Sharon, since on the way I was far too nervous to chit-chat and all my replies to her had been short, one-word answers. She told me about her past with drugs, and that she'd done so much damage to her body that she was declared fully disabled by the state. But she'd changed her life and now spent much of her time volunteering in different ways since she couldn't work. One of those ways was driving for this rehab, which she did multiple times a week.

Sharon was joyful. She laughed a lot and made plenty of lighthearted jokes to ease the tension, saying that even the most serious situations didn't require us to be in a bad mood. I liked her a lot and looked forward to the next time she'd give me a ride somewhere.

Once I started the routine of the new program, I realized that it was not like any of the others I had been in before. The inpatient portion of the "rehab" was on a floor level of an apartment complex in the heart of the city. Our floor was broken apart by hallways, keeping the men and women separated by a long corridor, but the other floors housed regular renters, not rehab participants. There were four women in a two-bedroom unit and no supervision overnight, from what I could tell.

The apartment was newer, with shiny appliances and quartz countertops. Every morning, we would meet downstairs and wait for the van to show up that would drive us through the busy LA streets to the high-rise corporate building that Brandon had taken me to that first day. The next eight hours would be spent in a program—meaning therapy sessions, recovery classes teaching us how to get and stay clean, and open-share groups for discussion about our lives and why we wanted to change them. The materials were pretty standard, but I wasn't used to the amount of freedom they offered, and it was obvious that the rest of the ladies took full advantage of that freedom.

While my intentions were good, it was easy to fall into the routine of whatever was happening around me. If the other ladies were sneaking out after the business day was done to hang out with the normies a few floors down, I'd go with them. I even smoked weed with them a few times because I knew that weed stays in the system for at least thirty days. Although testing positive for any harder substances would have meant I couldn't remain at the facility, marijuana was an exception, as it could still show up on a test weeks after last use, making it easier to explain away. I was always able to create a compromise with myself and still move forward as if I was doing the right thing.

Bending or even blatantly breaking the rules was second nature to me. I had no gauge for where a line was crossed or where it became blurry. In my own mind, I was on a new path. I was changing my life. I was doing the right thing, because the wrong thing was so much more extreme than leaving the apartment for a few hours or smoking a little dirt weed. My moral compass was completely skewed, and I truly believed I was doing well in that program, despite my secret rule breaking.

I still showed up promptly to the van every morning and followed the rules set before me, at least when people were watching. I made some good progress while I was there, for the most part. I asked Sharon to be my recovery sponsor and got along well enough with the other residents. Brandon had already written to me and I had responded. Because I went through most of my coming down in the motel, I didn't have the misery of withdrawal distracting me every day. Thirty days later, when my court date came around, Melanie drove me and acted as the formal representative from the program.

I can't remember the exact emotions I felt sitting in the courtroom that day, waiting to hear my fate. I'm not sure if I blocked them out, if I'd gone completely numb at the time, or if I was just shellshocked by the whole experience. I did have a public defender for this court appearance, a thin gentleman with curly brown hair who wore a brown suit and a brown tie. I hadn't been to court outside of the cage very often, so when he invited me to join him in a small, soundless room to the side, it caught me a little off guard. I went in and sat across from him while he reviewed my file.

"So, Miss Harris, you missed your check in with probation, which was a requirement of your joint suspension, and he issued warrants," he said while looking down at the pages in front of him. "However, you admitted yourself into a rehabilitation facility in Los Angeles. It looks like your probation officer has recommended that you be allowed to stay at the rehab—that's good, that's good. This all looks fine. Do you have a letter from the rehabilitation center with you?"

"I have a letter, but also my case manager is here with me, sitting against the back wall."

"Oh, that's even better. Have a seat with her and wait for the judge to call your case. We are going to ask that you be allowed to stay at the rehab. It's a 50/50 shot, but that's all we've got."

I sat in the room and watched as case after case was called. I watched as inmates walked up to the gate and spoke into the tiny microphone, as people in the courtroom thinned out a few at a time, and as each verdict was given while impatiently waiting for my turn.

When the judge finally called my name, I shuddered on the inside.

The judge was an older man with white hair that made a soft ring around the back of his head and creases of age etched into his face. I'd had this judge before, although I doubted he remembered me among all the faces he usually saw from one day to the next.

"Ms. Harris, the defense is requesting that we do not pull your extended sentence today, despite the fact that you didn't call your probation officer or seek permission to leave the county for rehab. Your probation officer has recommended the same. The DA disagrees and believes you've had as many chances as you deserve. So, in situations such as these, it's my job to determine who is correct, do you understand?"

"Yes, sir."

"Because of your extensive criminal history and the lack of legitimate consequences, I have determined that the DA does pose a valid point: that you have exhausted the energies of this court system to try and find a foundational solution and have continued to take the chances we have given you for granted. But I do take the recommendations of probation very seriously. They are the ones who work with you face to face, and if yours says to leave you in rehab, then I suppose that is a valuable opinion.

The court has decided to sentence you to the full two-year joint suspension sentence, pending the completion of the program you're currently in. You will maintain contact with your probation officer, and we will calendar you for another court appearance in three months. Should you return to court having not completed the required time at this facility, you will be remanded and given the full sentence, understood?"

"Yes, sir, thank you." My mouth said yes, but my mind didn't exactly understand what had just happened. I think I zoned out after the first few sentences, so I had no idea if I was about to have cuffs placed on my wrists or not.

The public defender explained it in simpler terms. Go back to rehab, don't leave, and come back to court in three months. If I didn't complete the program, I would go to prison for the full two years.

That felt like the best-case scenario right then. While I can't say I felt entirely free from the extended sentence, I did feel pretty confident that I could complete five more months at this rehab and at least get back in good standings with the court. Given my track record with rehab, I'm not sure what made me think I'd be able to do it this time. Maybe the time I'd spent with Brandon had influenced me, maybe I was more afraid of prison than I thought, or maybe I really was ready for a new chapter and journey in my life.

Whatever it was, I rode back from court that day feeling hopeful, proud even, of the determination I had to go back to the court in three months with a good report.

REFLECT

Once again, a single decision changed the entire trajectory of my life. In a moment so fleeting that I don't even remember it happening, I altered the journey into the next phase of my life drastically. It's a reminder of how important it is to consider our steps before we take them, recognizing that decisions have consequences. Many of us are always one bad decision away from ending up in front of a judge, having no place to live, or losing all the things we've worked so hard for, and we don't even realize it.

The respect I showed my probation officer was valuable and reciprocated. I believe he saw something in me that I wasn't able to see in myself. He treated me as the person he knew I could be and not the person I was. With people in positions of authority, it always proved more beneficial as an inmate and as a person to show decency and kindness instead of attitude and rebelliousness. Every person I met who was disrespectful and arrogant pushed themselves into having more issues instead of less.

This is true no matter what person of authority we are dealing with—teachers, employers, parents. Being respectful to the person leading us will always bring us a better outcome than disrespect. Of course, not every person in authority will show us that same level of respect in return, but that is usually an issue of their heart, not ours.

Every action has a reaction. Every choice has a consequential outcome, whether bad or good. Positioning ourselves to stop bending the rules to suit our own agenda will always take us closer to the ultimate goal.

REFLECTIVE QUESTIONS

1. Life is full of choices, and sometimes we only see the consequences
    in hindsight. Describe a time when you had two options and you
    ended up picking the wrong one. What was the outcome?

    _____

    _____

    _____

    _____

2. Respect isn't always earned. Sometimes we give it automatically
    based on someone's role or position. Do you find it easy or difficult
    to show respect to authority figures? What kind of personal growth
    could help you in that area?

    _____

    _____

    _____

    _____

3. Do you believe that rules are a necessary part of life and society?
    Are there any rules that you're comfortable bending or breaking?
    Which ones do you think you should start following?

    _____

    _____

    _____

    _____

Chapter 9
Standing on the Edge

"After all, a homeless man has reason to cry,
everything in the world is pointed against him."

~ Jack Kerouac

A few days after court, Sandra and Melanie rounded up all the residents, male and female, into the van and drove us to a park down the street. Once we unloaded, they separated us by gender, with the male counselors taking the guys and Sandra leading the ladies over to some picnic tables to sit down. We all waited in anticipation, as Melanie and Sandra seemed to be preparing an announcement.

"Well, we know this isn't our normal programming, but something has come up, and we want to make sure to tell you all sooner rather than later. Now I don't want anyone to panic—we are going to find solutions for everyone—but our facility has officially lost its funding for our inpatient services. We have always been transparent about not taking money from residents and that instead, our program is primarily county funded. But the county has decided to cut some programs and unfortunately, ours is one of them."

Sandra was soft but direct when delivering this news to us. The gasps and sighs of the women started to build as she continued to speak louder to regain our attention.

"We will still receive funding for our day program, so eight hours of classes will still be available to everyone Monday through Thursday. All of you are still enrolled and compliant, but everyone will need to find a new place to live. We do have resources available for those of you who don't have any other options, and we will not close our doors until we are sure every one of you has a place to stay." She finished.

As I listened to her words, I didn't make a sound. I just felt the weight of complete uncertainty hit my chest. I had just been ordered by the court to stay in this program. I was still miles away from anyone I knew. All the other programs in the county had already denied me access because of my lack of food stamps. My mind immediately started an internal search for a solution that could get me out of this situation, but the only ideas I could come up with involved going back on the run and basically signing off on my own two-year prison sentence.

I think Sandra could somehow see what was happening inside my head, because she came up and placed her hand on my shoulder as soon as she was done speaking.

"We are going to figure this out, please don't worry," she said.

"I literally have nowhere to go, like no other option. And what about the court? They just sentenced me to two years if I don't stay here. I don't wanna go to prison and…" I rambled on, the pitch of my voice getting higher with each word until she interrupted.

"Hey, hey, hey, stop. I am not going to abandon you. We will figure this out. You are still in this program, and you're going to finish it strong. You need to have faith that it will work out. Have faith, Kelsey. God brought you here. He will keep you here."

I nodded as we started walking back to the van, but I couldn't say her words lightened my anxiety very much. I felt like so many people wanted me to have faith and put my trust in a God that I wasn't even certain I understood or believed in. They spoke as if I could just con-jure up this feeling and my problems would disappear, requiring no deeper understanding of what those words really meant. To me, they were just more words. I started to wonder how someone who possessed faith behaved differently than someone who did not in situations such as this one.

I knew that I had no other choice than to trust that Sandra would be able to pull some strings or move some things around to get me somewhere to stay. And I was a survivor, able to stand back up after life knocked me down time and time again. This time was no different. So, for the moment, I rested on that.

After the news was delivered, we had about a week to plan for our departure from the apartment complex. Some of the girls were going home to their families, some found other facilities to take them, but myself and one other lady, Beverly, were in similar positions. We had to wait quietly for someone else to have full control of our lives and tell us where we'd be living next. We continued our daily programming as one by one, everyone left.

Once we were the last two residents still in the building, Sandra called Beverly and I into the office and told us that she'd found housing for us together at the same place. She explained that the facility would provide us with food, shelter, and weekly bus tokens. We would ride the bus back and forth to the high rise each day to keep our status as residents of the program, even though we'd be living offsite.

I was relieved that someone would be going to this new mystery place with me. When we packed up the next morning for our new destina-tion, I felt calm, believing that things would work out. Sandra had done what she'd promised, and I valued and appreciated the way that she had become someone I could trust. I was feeling pretty ready to transition to this new place, until I stepped out of the car for the very first time and onto the streets of Skid Row, Los Angeles.

I was raised in Las Vegas and too caught up in my own drama to pay attention to much else since moving to California, so I had no idea what Skid Row was or that such a place even existed. As I climbed out of the van, the very first thing I saw was a man smoking a crack pipe on the side of the road, right out in the open. There were tents lining each side of the street in every direction that I could see, and trash piled up on every corner. People covered in dirt and desperation meandered through the streets aimlessly, and others yelled and cursed at the air in front of them. Scantily-clad women walked through the crowd while men who leaned against the brick walls gawked at them. I took all of this in rapidly, in just the two minutes it took for Melanie to park, climb out of the van, and walk us inside a large building that sat right in the middle of what felt like an entirely different planet.

We followed Melanie into the lobby of the Weingart Center. Once we entered, a security guard stopped us. He picked up a phone that sat behind a counter and said a few words, letting whoever was on the other end know that we were there, then gave us directions to the elevator and the correct floor.

We stepped out of the elevator into bright fluorescent lights that ricocheted off white linoleum floors. Brown doorways stretched out in each direction and what looked like offices sat straight ahead. The walls were stamped with black-and-white door signs indicating the names of the inhabitants. For a second it reminded me of the waiting room that Barbara and Adam visited in *Beetlejuice* when they wanted to get the living out of their house, except more brightly lit.

A tall, bald man stepped out of one of the offices and greeted Melanie with a handshake and a gentle smile. It seemed like they knew each other in some way, or maybe they possessed a respect for one another and their chosen career paths that led them to places like this one, trying to help people like us as we struggled to help ourselves. The man ushered all of us into his office. Beverly and I sat while Melanie stood behind us.

"Ladies, it's nice to meet you. My name is Mark, and I'm one of the counselors here who will be helping you get settled in. I know this shift probably feels a little overwhelming, but we are ready to assist in meeting your individual needs and keeping you focused on finishing your outpatient program. Once the program is complete, we offer plenty of services here to help you find jobs, transitional living opportunities, and other resources you may need. We do have rules and requirements for you to stay in this shelter, so once we show you your rooms and let Melanie go, we can go over what some of those are and how to best manage your time here. Sound good?"

No. It did not sound good. I did not want to stay there. I had no idea where I was and felt entirely out of control of my own circumstances. Everything inside of me wanted to stand right back up and walk right back out, but the sensible part of my brain recognized that it would be a dead-end decision. So instead, I nodded and smiled, keeping any discomfort or other emotions tucked safely inside me like I always did.

Even though the inside of the homeless shelter wasn't as bad as the outside, I knew I would have to go past the outside to get to the bus that would take me to the program. I didn't want to go back out there. When Mark showed me to my room, similar in size to the cell I had lived in off and on for the past four years, I thanked him and set my things down gently on the small bed. Suddenly I regretted my decision to trust Sandra. I was wishing I had lied and said I had somewhere to go and just figured things out on my own again like I always had.

Of course, those thoughts had to stay hidden. I had to keep my game face on and stay strong. As Melanie hugged us goodbye before heading to the elevator, I smiled and assured her that I was okay. I was always okay.

After I met with Mark and learned the rules of my new place of residence, I joined Beverly, the only person I knew, for dinner at the cafeteria next door. I allowed myself to embrace the level of comfort she seemed to have. I don't want to say that I was afraid, because I didn't feel that way. Out of place, uncomfortable, on high alert—those words seem to describe the way living on Skid Row felt in the beginning more than being *afraid* does.

After a few days of a routine there though, I kind of started to adapt to the environment. Living on Skid Row was one thing, but getting clean there was a whole other animal. Walking past so many people daily who had succumbed to their addictions while trying to keep my eyes set straight ahead on the goal of completing the program and therefore staying out of prison was like walking on a tightrope without a net beneath me. After a few days, I didn't even see the drugs anymore, all I saw was the desperation and insanity that the drugs created.

I called my mom and told her what had happened at the rehab, and that I'd be living in a homeless shelter until I was able to complete the outpatient program. She was surprised and voiced some concern about where I was, but she never said she'd come get me out. My aunt and uncle even came to take me to lunch shortly after I arrived, and they saw with their own eyes where I was living. They gave me a twenty-dollar bill and dropped me back off at the shelter, and they made no mention of helping me find a different solution that wasn't in such a dangerous area. I was grateful they had come, but I couldn't help but wonder why they didn't even try to take me home with them instead of leaving me there.

I hadn't always considered myself to be homeless, despite the obvious fact that I didn't have somewhere I could return to when needed. The first time I realized that I didn't have an actual place to call home was when I returned to my cell after court once and read through the yellow sheets of paper they handed me with my minutes on it. The papers showed that the district attorney had recommended house arrest for whatever crime I had committed that time, and that my public defender had declined. On the line where it asked for a reason, the lawyer had typed the word TRANSIENT in bold letters.

Since I didn't live in a tent, or beg for food, or hold a cardboard sign, I didn't see myself as a transient. I was almost always able to find a shower, a place to store my things, or a party house to crash at. I had slept on couches, on the floor in closets, and in kidsize beds. I had squatted in empty houses, lived in sheds in backyards, or slept in the beds of men who would give theirs up in anticipation of getting something in return. Sometimes, I even gave it to them to maintain the lie that I told myself: I always had somewhere to go. Now, things didn't feel the same. For the first time, I felt like the title of *transient* truly fit.

I reflected on how I'd thought my rock-bottom moment was sitting in front of that donut shop and how now, sitting in the midst of what it really looked like to exchange everything for your addictions, knowing I had put myself there, knowing that I had no one who cared enough about me to help me escape this current situation—suddenly, that felt like the real bottom of the rock.

The realization that I had done this to myself struck me deeply. I had pushed everyone who loved me away and chosen my drugs for years. What right did I have to think any of them should rescue me now? I knew I was standing on the edge, somewhere between seeking a different life and giving up entirely. At just twenty-seven years old, having only been out of jail for two months, I considered the possibility of letting it end there.

I could see how easy it would be to slip into this world with everyone else and vanish into the sea of tents. I could see how no one would try and save me from my own personal annihilation, if that was the choice I made. I could see how releasing the pressure of trying to keep my sanity here and, instead, joining in with those who had already lost their minds could be freeing. But I didn't do any of that.

Instead, I got clean. For real this time.

I woke up every day and took my backpack and my token to the bus and rode it to the corporate building for the day program. I met with Sharon and went over the twelve steps with her. I met a few people living on the same floor as me and went to some of the recovery events that the shelter offered, walked to the NA meetings at the park down the street as the building required, and visited the cafeteria twice a day for my free meals. I followed the rules as best I could, stuck to the curfew, and did what they told me to do.

I met a lot of interesting people on the streets of Skid Row. There was a gangster who called himself Trojan who wore dark shades at night and a different purple shirt every day. He took a liking to me, and he would often show up outside the door of the shelter in the morning and at the bus stop in the evening to walk with me, while hoping I would take a liking to him too. He was well-groomed and admired, and he did not have the appearance of someone who should frequent these streets as often as he did. I have to assume his reason for being there and spending time walking with me was not built on good intentions.

There was a group of people that often hung out in front of the shelter where I lived who befriended me. They were men and women who didn't even use hard drugs, but who had abandoned the rules of society with a sound mind and chosen the unhoused life instead. They had a deep desire to avoid the pursuit of the "American Dream" and didn't want to pay taxes or listen to *the man*. So they lived on the streets and embraced a different kind of freedom.

They didn't care about the dirt under their fingernails or strive for luxuries like heat or running water, which we so often take for granted. They were perfectly content with the little they had. These were some of the happiest people I've ever met, and they inspired a certain peace and acceptance of my circumstances that I don't believe I would have had if I hadn't met them.

I also saw things on Skid Row that were deeply disturbing and hard to process. I walked down the street toward the bus stop once and could hear what sounded like a rape happening inside a zipped up tent, right in the middle of the day. The woman's feet stuck out of the tent, and I paused and watched in horror as people stepped around them and past the shaking fabric while ignoring the screams coming from inside. Eventually, I stepped around it too.

I participated in Narcotics Anonymous meetings around the neighborhood at different shelters, as required. The front of one particular shelter would normally have people sprawled out on every inch of pavement available, hoping that they could hold their spot long enough to be first in line when the sun went down. As I walked through the courtyard of this shelter one afternoon to attend a meeting inside, I stepped past a young woman with a baby on her lap. Right behind the head of the child, I saw an open flame flickering against the glass of a pipe full of crack cocaine. The mother inhaled, then blew smoke inches from the child's face.

I spent a lot of time in my room at the shelter. A neighbor on my floor level gave me a small TV with a built-in DVD player that I propped up on a broken plastic chair and set in front of my bed. I would often walk down to the library and rent shows on DVD that I would hide in my room and watch for hours on the weekends when there was no outpatient program to attend.

One day, as I lay on my small bed watching an episode of *Lost* on the small screen, I heard a commotion in the hallway that caught my attention. The gasps and shouts forced me out of my solitude, and I went to see what was happening.

"I think she's dead, oh my God. She's my best friend, I can't go in there," a small Hispanic woman said through panicked tears. She had a short, spiked haircut and was covered in tattoos that sagged with her aging skin.

She stood outside a brown door that belonged to a young lady I had spoken to several times since I moved in. She was maybe thirty-five years old, with curly blonde hair, round rosy cheeks, and a friendly smile. She was a bit on the heavier side, and I'd witnessed the brief cruelty she endured because of that more than once.

As I stood at my door watching the crowd of people grow in size across the hall, the short Hispanic woman looked towards me and spoke.

"Will you check on her please? She said you were nice to her. Please, I don't want any of these jerks to touch her—" hostility rose in her voice as she looked around, clenching her fists, "but she might need help. The ambulance is coming, but will you please go in and see if she's alive?"

I nodded and stepped out into the hall, walking over to the room across from me. The Hispanic woman gently touched my arm as I went past the group of onlookers and into the room of her best friend.

The woman was laying on her stomach in a white tank top and cheap underwear, a small glimmer of drool seeping from her bluish-colored lips. I knelt beside her and touched her shoulder to try and shake her awake, but her skin felt cold against my fingers.

I looked out at her friend in the hallway and indicated that I thought we were too late. But her eyes held such anticipation that I looked back toward the girl and tried to turn her over instead. She was too heavy for me to move, and despite my best efforts, all I was able to do was check for a pulse in the folds of her neck that I never found.

"I'm sorry, I think she's dead," I said gently as I struggled to pull a blanket out from under her to try and cover her almost-naked body.

"Will you please just sit with her? I can't go in there, but I don't want her to be all alone while we wait." Her words were broken up through sobs.

I nodded and sat down on the chair right beside the body, not really sure what I should do with my hands. I was probably there about ten minutes before the first responders arrived. They asked me a few brief questions, then waved me out of the room.

It wasn't the first time I had encountered a dead body, but it certainly felt different. Now that I wasn't numbed by toxins or distracted by the chaos around me, I could actually understand the heaviness of this young life being lost, and the weight of the grief that her best friend was experiencing.

Death on Skid Row was frequent and usually sudden, though I imagine it's something to be expected in lifestyles such as these. The black coroner's van was often seen pulled over on the side of the road, with a shiny black bag being removed from whichever tent or shelter housed the soulless body this time. I would sometimes wonder about the life that was lost, but more often I would wonder about the men and women whose job it was to remove the bodies. I wondered if they were still impacted by each one, or if the faces all started to blur together after a while, like the faces of the living did for me some days.

REFLECT

Having faith in someone or something other than myself was difficult for me. I had always been a survivor, navigating through life's challenges on my own and believing with full certainty that the only person I could count on was me. So, when faith in God kept being brought up to me again and again, I struggled with understanding why having it was so important. I believed that my ability to survive was based solely on me and nothing else. Attempting to *have faith* took a new kind of courage for me, and I tiptoed toward it with no expectations.

If you've been a believer for a long time, these words hold a deeper value and meaning to you, but for those who are stepping into it for the first time, the lack of an explanation for what faith is or how to harness it can be confusing and sometimes overwhelming.

Once I found myself in a place like Skid Row, believing I'd been abandoned and forgotten, I felt even more certain that God was not journeying toward helping me with anything. It was easy for me to shake off the idea of a loving God and continue forward as though I was in complete control. I didn't realize that the time I spent standing on the edge was by design, to show me up close exactly where I was headed if I didn't change.

What's interesting about that is that Skid Row was basically created by Christians. Train crews would lay over for the upcoming railroad expansions. Eventually, soldiers that had come back from serving in World War II and later, Vietnam, would find themselves with nowhere to go. They would ride the train to LA and land there, forming a small tent city that would become the hub for shelters and other faith-based resources.

In time, that small area continued to grow. By the time I got there, it stretched fifty-four square blocks, and the inhabitants changed from wandering soldiers to the mentally ill, physically addicted, and socially abandoned. When I arrived, it no longer seemed to retain the feeling of hope that I imagine those early Christians held for those sacrificial soldiers so long ago. Instead, it felt like a drop-off zone for the unloved and seemingly unlovable.

Witnessing the type of heaviness that exists on Skid Row was a profound experience for me. I learned that there is a whole world within that neighborhood that functions in a unique way, built by tragedy and the surrender to one's own vices. I believe that it does a disservice to society for us to not know what is happening in places like this. These people are human just like the rest of us. They are someone's daughter, son, mother, or brother living on these streets. And slowly they become faceless, losing their identity to their own disillusionment. And we press on, pretending that they aren't there.

REFLECTIVE QUESTIONS

1. "Having faith" means different things to different people, depending on your background or beliefs. What does faith mean to you personally? Would you say you live like someone who has faith? Why or why not?

     _____

     _____

     _____

     _____

2. Self reliance matters, but it doesn't mean we should never accept help. Describe a time when you felt like you had no one to rely on but yourself. What led to that and how did you handle it?

     _____

     _____

     _____

     _____

3. Areas like Skid Row exist in cities all over the world, often marked
    by poverty and struggle. Have you ever visited a place like this?
    What was that experience like for you, and how did it affect you
    emotionally or mentally?

    _____

    _____

    _____

    _____

Chapter 10
Lapsing in Judgement

"Don't mourn over your bad decisions.
Just start overcoming them with good ones."

~ Joyce Meyer

As my days in downtown LA continued to pass, I started to feel a little complacent. Whenever I was clean for a while in the past, the numbness that I had always gotten through illicit drugs would almost immediately be replaced with a prescription for some type of an antidepressant. This time was no different. The psych at the homeless shelter met with me for five minutes, heard that I'd always taken Prozac, and wrote me a script for that.

I was sixteen years old when I was prescribed pills for the first time, after being released from the ER following a botched "suicide attempt." While I don't think I would have minded if an overdose took me out, I stood firm that I was just trying to get some sleep after too many days of staying up partying, and that I overdid it on the Tylenol PM. But the doctors at the hospital refused to take that as an explanation for the hives that covered my body and the need for a charcoal cocktail. They let me go home with my mother but not without a promise that I would see a therapist and a psychiatrist.

I was eventually stamped with diagnoses like PTSD, Borderline Personality Disorder, and Intermittent Explosive Disorder. Most of the time, when the behaviors associated with these disorders would strike, I was coming down from drugs, while struggling to process the inevitable onset of traumatic triggers that I had so successfully hidden away with narcotics.

The early days of med experimentation were tough on me. I'm sure the fact that I sustained my use of methamphetamines as we swapped Effexor for Lexapro then Paxil didn't help. We finally landed on fluoxetine (Prozac), and this pill would zap me of any of the life I had left over after whatever the meth had already taken. I would appreciate the subtle way the depression would evaporate, but I always hated it after a few months, when the numbness would be too much even for me, and I would become a total zombie.

While I have always held strong opinions about the pharmaceutical industry and their impact on the recovery and addiction community, I still recognize the need for some of us to utilize medications for a while as we work through the pieces of our mind that need to be repaired. I count the diagnoses that I was labeled with as true at the time they were given to me, but I never believed that a diagnosis defined me. Many of the traumas that lived in my mind created the behaviors that would be considered borderline or explosive. For a long time, I wasn't able to stop those thoughts or behaviors without some form of medical assistance.

However, after a couple of months on Skid Row, clean from meth but numbed by Prozac, I decided one day on a whim that I didn't feel like taking medication anymore, so I stopped. Just like that.

Anyone who has been on these types of meds knows that stopping abruptly can have hazardous consequences. In my case, that's what happened. I had a minor meltdown, smashed a mirror, and proceeded to cut up my arms with the broken glass. It had been a long time since I'd injured myself, but it still didn't feel that strange to me to have cuts and marks all along my arms. I knew this wasn't something normal though, and that I would need to keep it hidden.

Using self-harm as a remedy for an outburst or mania started when I was a freshman in high school and in the middle of a very brief goth phase. My best friend and I were sitting in her room one day, and she pulled out a small tin box that was designed to store mints but instead it housed fresh razor blades, large safety pins, sewing needles, and a lighter to burn the bacteria off the sharp edges. I'm not sure what it was about inflicting physical pain on myself that appealed to me. As my adolescence passed, the goth phase faded but the self-harm stuck.

The cutting got so scary for my little sister throughout our younger years that there were times when she would hide anything sharp in our house from me, forcing us to cut up our dinner with butter knives and take razors out of the bathroom after every shower. While most people thought of cutting as attention seeking or a mediocre cry for help, she saw it as a genuine danger.

It is hard for me to describe the way the physical pain reduced the emotional pain. I think for me it allowed a quick release of all that I was holding inside to seep out of the open skin with the tiny spots of blood. The emotions were too big and too intense, but the cuts were small and manageable—something trivial that I could control.

After the mirror incident, I did my best to hide the treacherous marks on my arms with long sleeves and careful movements. But someone spotted the scabbed lines one day and reported them to Mark.

"Kelsey, this is a very serious matter. Self-harm puts you at risk for infection, and we can't permit someone with suicidal ideation to continue to live on the premises. We have to get you professional help," he said, after summoning me into his office one afternoon.

"I'm not suicidal at all. Cutting has nothing to do with suicide."

"Well, I won't pretend to understand it. Your file shows that you're taking medication for depression, and you've had multiple diagnoses since you were young. I know you're seeing our psychiatrist here, but I'd like you to start seeing our therapist as well."

He pulled out a pen and began to write the information for the therapist on a square of paper. "I am also giving you a written warning, if anything like this happens again, you may not be able to continue your time here. Please head down to her office now to get scheduled with her."

I nodded, took the small paper, and left the office.

I made my way to the elevator and noticed that the therapist's office was in the basement, which kept the whispers of the mentally sick down beneath the building floors so as not to distract from the day-to-day tasks that the homeless needed to focus on.

The therapist had a salt-and-pepper pixie haircut, small spectacles, and a large cardigan that hung off her tiny arms. She was fun and spunky, and she listened to me when I told her that I really didn't think that I wanted to live my life under a plethora of diagnoses in a pill-induced haze. I explained that I had used methamphetamines and other drugs during every psych evaluation I'd ever had, and for the first time in my life, I wanted to see what it was like to actually feel something.

She agreed that I could slowly taper off the Prozac and see what happened, as long as I did so under her care, meeting with her at least twice a week.

Her other stipulation was that I make a friend—someone I felt that I could trust and spend time with outside of my tiny room, and who didn't live in a tent in front of the homeless shelter. I didn't like the idea, but I agreed. Thus began my search for someone to connect with.

Friends made me nervous, especially there. I saw friendships as mostly transactional and, in this environment, there was nothing I really had to give or wanted to get.

The friend I made was a beautiful Black woman in her fifties named Vee. She wore dazzling green contacts in her eyes and long locs that fell down her back. Vee had lost her husband and eventually her home in another state, and she had moved to LA to start a new life. The move wasn't as easy as she thought it would be, and eventually the only place she could find to go was the same homeless shelter that I lived in. Vee spoke confidently and walked proudly, and she had big dreams she was sure would come to fruition. I was glad that she became my friend.

We would spend most of our time together in the cafeteria or walking around downtown. Once a month, when our General Relief reloaded onto our cards, we would walk the few blocks out of Skid Row and into the heart of Los Angeles, where we'd have to stretch our necks back to look up at the tall buildings and rub elbows with men and women in suits and shiny shoes in order to pass by them.

It was odd to me that the most populated homeless area in the country was less than a fifteen-minute walk from one of the richest parts of the world, but we used that to our advantage. We'd enter one of the high-rise buildings, take the elevator to the rooftop restaurant, and pretend our lives were different. We'd order an appetizer and drink water out of wine glasses while we looked down over the city, believing for just a little while that we belonged there instead.

I made friends with two other young ladies as well, and they would invite me to tag along to some of the things they did for fun. One of them was an ex-prostitute trying to change her ways, and the other had aged out of the foster care system, tried to make it on her own, and needed a little help while she figured out her next steps. They liked to attend the gatherings that the church across the street held and started to bring me with them. There would be dancing and singing, fruit punch and desserts. Dancing to the electric slide with a group of homeless drug addicts in a rundown church in downtown LA was a whole new way to party for me, but I adjusted to it the best I could.

These same girls invited me to join them at a men's rehab facility for a Fourth of July barbecue. Since I wasn't doing anything else, I agreed. As I was standing outside waiting to meet them, I saw a couple passing by. The man was in a wheelchair, and the woman had her arms full of blankets and bags. Since they appeared to be struggling, and I had been on a friend-finding journey, I offered to give them a hand. She handed me a few items, and I followed them back into the shelter and to their room. I walked in and stood facing the man, chatting, while she moved around behind me. As I was preparing to walk out of the room, she tapped me on the shoulder to hand me something. I glanced over and grabbed the item.

"For your help," she said as she stretched a mirror towards me with a line broken out already on the glass. I looked in my hand and found a rolled-up dollar bill.

It was as if instinct just took over. It was second nature. I didn't even think about it before the bill was in my nose and I was breathing in the crushed-up crystal meth. Right as the familiar burn started to trickle down the back of my throat, I realized what I had just done. And while on the inside I was stunned, on the outside, I thanked her then walked calmly to meet the girls and head to the barbecue.

Once the barbecue had ended and we'd made it back to the shelter, the reality of the severity of what I had done dawned on me. I started to stress over the likely consequences of that one swift moment where I lacked judgment and instinct had taken over. I assumed I'd be drug-tested, because it was a holiday and we'd been given a pass to leave the area for the day. I knew I would fail. Mark had already warned me after the self-harm incident that I was running low on second chances, and I had just blown it.

The next morning, a drug test was requested, as I'd predicted. I peed in the cup and left for the bus, my mind reeling about where I would go once the test came back dirty. I thought about the possibility that the drugs weren't even real since I hadn't really felt high at the barbecue at all. Maybe the test wouldn't be dirty. But the risk was too high.

The feeling that I couldn't have predicted, though, was guilt. I felt terrible about what I had done, and it was eating me up inside. I had come so far and worked so hard and now I'd thrown it away, after all the chances I'd been given and all the work I'd done to try to stay away from dope on those streets. I ended up asking for a phone call at the day program, calling Sharon and asking her to come meet me during a break to talk. She was there waiting when I walked out the door. I told her everything exactly as it happened, holding nothing back.

"Kelsey, this was not a relapse. This was a lapse. It was a lapse in judgment and now you're here, confessing what you did and getting right back to the program. I don't think you need to totally start over, but I do think you should sit down with Sandra and with Mark and tell them exactly what you just told me. Let the chips fall where they may. Part of recovery is accepting the consequences for our own actions."

Since I didn't want to lie, and I didn't want to leave, the suggestion she gave was the one that made the most sense.

To my surprise, Sandra was easy to confess to. She said the same thing that Sharon did. She expressed how proud she was of me that I'd immediately told the truth instead of trying to fake my way out of a dirty test and how it showed growth on my part. She agreed that it was a lapse and to keep my clean date the same, and she would back me up with the shelter if I needed her to.

Mark didn't go quite so easy on me though.

"Kelsey, I appreciate the courage it took for you to tell the truth to your day program and to me. But I have to ask, if I hadn't already drug-tested you, would you have even bothered?" he asked sternly.

"I don't know, I think I would have because I feel really bad, but I guess I won't ever know for sure."

"I think that's something you need to think about while you're here. Are you working an honest program or are you just trying to skate by and avoid prison? What you decide to do with your life is up to you, and you can make it easier on yourself or harder, but you can't continue to break the rules without consequences. There are people out there who are fighting for your space here, and you just took advantage of it, again."

"I understand, and I'm sorry, I really didn't plan this at all." I was sure he was about to tell me to pack up my things and get out. But he didn't. Instead he softened and kept speaking.

"I am going to move you out of your own room and onto the dorm floor. Maybe having more people around will help you stay a little more accountable to yourself and others. But this is it, no more chances," he said.

"I understand. Thanks, Mark," I said quietly. I made my way out of his office to begin packing up my small space to move to the dorm.

REFLECT

Self-harm is often a symptom of a much larger emotional struggle. Because it only affects less than 17% of the population, and often only teens and young adults, it seems to be a mystery to most people as to why it helps some of us to move through the emotional pain that we can't confront. It took a long time to understand my triggers, learn safe coping skills and walk through tough emotions. But after the mirror incident, I never (physically) self-harmed again. I also never took another medication for depression or any other disorder.

Medications are a tricky thing. It is my opinion that our society has been persuaded to lean on them instead of actively exploring what it is that is causing us to act out in the first place. While it can often be a chemical imbalance, I think it's just as likely that a lot of these disorders stem from unresolved trauma and the inability to truly understand what we are feeling and why. I would never tell anyone not to take medication that is truly needed, but I would encourage you to not stop there. A licensed therapist or counselor can help anyone to work on how emotional triggers may be the deeper cause of certain behaviors.

The correlation between stopping all medications and finding a friend seems interesting but not all that surprising. If we really think about it, many of us struggle with isolation, feeling different from other people, and not being able to open up about what we're experiencing. The therapist wanted me to find someone that I could lean on and talk to during a unique time in my life, and doing that did help me in a lot of ways. Of course, the journey to find a friend eventually led me to a huge lapse in judgement that could have cost me greatly.

People need people. We were not created to spend our lives all alone. But the process of choosing which people we surround ourselves with is just as important as finding a good therapist or program. We can't always take giant leaps towards new people without having an idea of the kind of life they live. We have to be diligent in protecting ourselves and monitoring our surroundings. Quality friendships are vital to our growth as not only recovering addicts, but also human beings. But we need protective boundaries in place when bringing new people into our lives.

REFLECTIVE QUESTIONS

1. There are many healthy ways to cope, but without knowing about them, some people turn to harmful behaviors. Have you ever used any form of self-harm as a way to cope? If not, what other unhealthy coping strategies have you used?

    _____

    _____

    _____

    _____

2. Having someone to lean on and confide in is truly invaluable. Name three people that you would consider to be that kind of friend. What qualities make them reliable and trustworthy?

    _____

    _____

    _____

    _____

3. We read about my sponsor describing what happened in the shelter as a lapse, not a relapse. In your opinion, what's the difference between a lapse and a relapse? Do you believe that distinction matters?

    _____

    _____

    _____

    _____

Chapter 11
Bonding in Trauma

"She thirsted for love but found only a mirage.
Some hearts are a desert you can die wandering in."

~ John Mark Green

*B*eing forced to move out of my own room and into a dorm room was a harsher punishment than it seemed when Mark was handing it out to me. The space I now lived in was not much bigger than the room I was in before. With two sets of bunk beds and three other women, it quickly overwhelmed me. The hustle and bustle on this floor was a vast difference from the tiny, silent sanctuary of my old room. Ironically, the constant chatter reminded me of how solitary confinement felt in the county jail.

I was happy to be on the same floor as Vee now. I was less than thrilled that I would be required to attend all the events that were put on by the shelter that I was previously allowed to skip. The upcoming event was considered black-tie, where dresses and gowns were brought in. They ushered us in for fittings and to receive elaborate hairstyles. It seems absurd that in the middle of this island of the addicted and mentally ill, small named-celebrities and other LA elites would throw things like black-tie events. I actually assumed that they either got some kind of twisted enjoyment out of it, or they thought being in the same room as them would somehow give us a newfound motivation to elevate our social status.

This was so wildly outside of my comfort zone that I felt like the punishment for my lapse just kept on giving. I had never been one to draw attention to myself with fancy clothes. I didn't feel qualified to wear nice dresses or participate in functions such as this. But I chose my dress, a floor length, burgundy V-neck halter with beads on the straps, let them put my hair into an up-do, donned some dangly earrings, and went to the event.

The event itself wasn't too memorable, but on the walk back, my friend and I were approached by two men who would turn out to be hard to forget.

"Well, look at you. You ladies look way too nice to be out here on these streets. What party did we miss?" one of them asked, directing his comment more toward my friend than to me. He was tall and bald, wearing a baggie basketball jersey and jeans that bunched around the ankles of his shoes.

While they began to chat, I slowly made eye contact with the man standing next to him. He was also tall, wearing a white tank top that showed a small tattoo on his bicep, and his light blue eyes caught my attention instantly. His name was Ethan, and he resembled every man I'd ever been attracted to. As the conversations progressed, I found that he fit my type perfectly. Handsome, not too bright, and on parole.

The romantic relationships that I'd formed in the midst of an addictive lifestyle were always chaotic and destructive in one way or another. I'd had my fair share of failed partnerships by this point, with issues that ranged from subtle misogyny and neglect to downright abusive and toxic behaviors.

There was Sean, an enigmatic bully with a darkness that covered his spirit so deeply that it showed on his face. He was in a relationship with someone else when we met, but the pull between us seemed magnetic, so fierce that neither of us could ignore it. He had a mean streak that went beyond yelling and physical fighting to a deep psychological manipulation. I would watch him use it on unsuspecting victims to get what he wanted before resorting to violence.

I'll admit that I was strangely attracted to this power he seemed to harness, and it would pull me closer to him, until he started using it on me. He went to the dark side so drastically that by the end of our relationship, I had woken up to him attempting to inject drugs into my arm while I slept. On another occasion, he became so possessive and fearful that he'd lose me during his trip to prison that he convinced a tattoo artist that owed him money to come to my hotel room and tattoo his name on me while he listened on the phone. The artist was so afraid of him that I allowed that fear to impact me as well. To this day, I carry his name, small but permanent, written on my chest.

There was also Jerry, who seemed fun and easygoing at first, but would end up revealing another side of himself that was mean and disrespectful. He locked me in a room for five hours once when he couldn't find his bag of dope (that ended up being under the bed). I broke up with him a few days later, so he shot at me in an alley at 3am. After that, he went full-blown stalker, showing up randomly wherever I was, dramatically trying to win me back. That relationship finally ended when he was arrested after being chased by the police, who followed him to an apartment where I was staying. When the police asked me if I knew him, I said no. As he was being hauled away, he shouted about how much he loved me from the back of the squad car.

Any other relationship I was a part of usually ended in cheating, incarceration—theirs or mine, a trade-off from one partner to another, or a slow fade of communication when I started to feel too bored or too threatened. Of course, I wasn't always the victim, but also the perpetrator—an emotionless Jezebel who would chew weaker men up and spit them back out if they weren't strong enough to deal with me.

There was a thin line between the strength that I sought in men and their ability to control me. I could always see how every man I attempted a relationship with reminded me of Mike (my son's father) in one way or another. How I would chase the way I felt about him with these other guys and never even come close to that feeling. My initial attraction to Ethan was no different.

Ethan was the typical victim of a societal letdown, having been in and out of incarceration since adolescence and never acquiring the skills or desire to try and live any differently. He had a quick wit and a silver tongue that the words flowed from with ease. He told us that he and his friend were both recently released from prison, didn't have an address to parole to, and were temporarily being housed in the same shelter that we currently resided in.

We stayed and chatted with them for a few more minutes, but as the curfew for the shelter was swiftly approaching, we had to rush off to make it inside the doors before they were locked until morning. The curfew there was strict—if you didn't make it back on time, you spent the whole night wandering the streets.

The next day, as I walked out of the dimly lit shelter and into the warm summer sun, Ethan was the first person I saw. His fresh white tee was blinding as he saw me too, and he walked over and joined me on the stroll down to the cafeteria and eventually the bus stop.

Our Skid Row romance was instant, even though right before we'd met, I'd been in a semi-talking stage with a Hispanic gangster who'd lost one of his legs in a gang-related shooting. Ethan and I were immediately inseparable. He was funny, charming, and protective. The ever-so-slight threat of being a young woman alone in a homeless shelter evaporated entirely when he was with me.

We talked a lot and laughed even more. We found cheap ways to go on dates and snuck into single rooms to be alone whenever we could. In retrospect, I'm not sure if this was falling in love or trauma bonding. I'm not even sure that it matters.

As time passed and we grew closer, the date approached for my three-month check in with the judge. I wasn't sure how this court visit would go since I was no longer a resident of my previous rehab, but an out-patient client instead. I distracted myself from my nerves by spending as much time with Ethan as I possibly could. My attention to my program waned a little. While I wasn't getting high, there were times where I questioned if Ethan was as clean as he said he was. I would suppress my suspicions and go about my business, preparing for a day trip to the courthouse.

When the day arrived, Ethan waited with me patiently for Melanie to pick me up from the front of the shelter. The anxiousness coming off me was palpable.

"You are going to be fine, babe. You're doing great out here, any judge will be able to see that," he said, giving my shoulder a slight squeeze.

"Thanks, I know I'm doing pretty good. It's just the idea of going to prison now seems so much harder for some reason," I replied.

"Well, that is obviously because you met me, and now you can't imagine a life without me in it," he said with a quick wink.

I rolled my eyes and looked away as Melanie pulled up. I squeezed Ethan's hand before I climbed into the car for the long drive to the courthouse.

The court visit proved to be far less eventful than I had worried it would be. The judge reviewed the letter from the rehab and the homeless shelter and spoke briefly with Melanie to confirm my participation in both. He accepted my change in address and ordered me to stay at the Weingart Center for at least the duration of my program, continue my outpatient treatment, and come back again in three more months. That timeframe would land right after my six months in the program were complete.

I was happy with the outcome, having slowly started to embrace my routine and feeling comfortable that the time I was spending with Ethan would get me through these last few months.

As the days continued to pass, I started to notice changes in Ethan more often than I had before. My suspicions that he was getting high while I was at my day program were all but confirmed one day when he showed up to the bus stop to meet me totally dazed and out of his mind. When I confronted him about it, he just laughed and walked away.

A few days later, Ethan didn't make it back to the shelter on time and lost his bed. A few days after that, he was kicked out of the program entirely. He still tried to stay nearby. I'm not sure where he would go overnight, but he would be there waiting for me every morning, right outside the shelter door.

"Kels, I can't do this anymore. Skid Row is kicking my butt, and I gotta get out of this area," he said to me one day, as we walked down the trash-covered sidewalk to the bus stop.

"I get it. It's hard out here with nowhere to stay."

"I talked to my sister. She has a place out in Orange County. She's coming to get me later today so I can go stay with her."

"Oh. Well, that's good. I really don't want you to leave, but I would have left a long time ago if I could,." I said, looking at the ground.

"Why don't you come with me? We can go stay with my sis for a little while then get our own place. You don't have to stay here."

"Ethan, I do have to stay here. I have that court case. The judge said I have to stay here until I finish the program, or I get the two-year sentence. I don't have that much time left. I can't go."

"Okay, well maybe after you finish that then," he said as the bus pulled up.

Leaving with Ethan did sound appealing. It took every logical thought I could muster up to tell him no and choose to stay in the shelter instead. I knew I risked him forgetting all about me once he was gone, but there was just too much at stake to leave now.

Later that day, his sister arrived as promised, excited to see her brother and take him home with her. She was friendly and funny, and I liked her right away, but I did feel a twinge of disappointment as I watched them driving off, once again leaving me all alone on Skid Row.

The first couple of weeks after Ethan left, we talked on the phone constantly. Hours of my time outside of the day program were spent in my room, with the phone plugged into the wall so I wouldn't have to hang up for any reason.

Having our relationship shift into primarily talking and nothing else forced us to get to know each other more and talk about real-life things. I had originally latched on to him out of attraction and protection, but as our conversations shifted, I started to actually like him. Eventually, though, the calls started to slow down and become shorter. I started to assume that I'd have to let him go sooner or later.

One day, as I stood outside the cafeteria after breakfast, Vee walked up to me and gave me a quick hug. She abruptly stepped back, a look of surprise covering her face.

"Girl, you're pregnant!" she said boldly.

"What?! No, I'm not. Why did you say that?"

"Girl, yes you are. I know what I know, and right now what I know is that there's a baby in you. You better go get a test and see, I ain't even playin'," she said as she continued walking.

It seemed crazy. But Vee sounded so confident, though I had no idea what made her feel that way, that I walked down to the liquor store and bought a cheap test, fully doubting that it would be positive. I sat in the homeless shelter bathroom, peed on the stick, and two minutes later, two bright red lines showed through on the white background.

I called Ethan later that day as I mentally prepared for him to freak out, tell me not to have it, or start yelling and cussing. But surprisingly, he didn't do any of that. Instead, he sounded genuinely excited, laughing and shouting about becoming a dad.

I, on the other hand, did not feel that same excitement. I felt numb, thoughtless, unable to process the situation with a sound mind. All I really knew was that the first step would be to go to a doctor for a con-firmation of the pregnancy. So I took the steps to find a clinic, make an appointment, and wait a few days until it came.

The day of the appointment, I slowly walked towards the clinic and was surprised to find Ethan coming forward to meet me. He had a huge grin on his face as he glided up and hugged me, the excitement of a new baby still in his voice and evident on his face.

"What are you doing here?" I asked through the hug.

"What do you mean? We're having a baby! I want to be here for all the important stuff, doctor appointments, all that."

"Well, that's sweet but this is nothing. They're probably just going to have me pee in a cup or something. You didn't have to come."

"I'm gonna be here for all of it, Kels. I also wanted to talk to you about something too, while we're in person."

When he said those words, he struggled to look me in the eye. I paused, waiting for what he was about to say.

"Look, I really do want to be here for our baby. Nothing will change that. But I don't want to be exclusive with you. I've been seeing someone else. She lives in the same complex as my sister. I just wanted to tell you the truth, so you don't get the wrong idea. But hey! We're having a baby!"

I wasn't sure what I was feeling besides the sting of rejection as I silently turned back toward the direction I was walking. He followed behind me, trying to keep up with my pace. I stayed quiet for a while, then turned back around.

"You know, Ethan, I'd rather you not come to this. You shouldn't have even come back here. I'm just going to do this by myself. You should go home," I said then turned back away from him.

He tried to argue for a minute and followed me another block or so. Eventually, he stopped and let me go, once he realized that I wasn't going to change my mind.

The appointment confirmed that I was pregnant, and when I got back to the shelter, he was gone.

REFLECT

Some men are trash, and relationships are really hard.

Is that the reality of the world, or is it what I learned from my own broken experiences and terrible taste in romantic prospects? In all honesty, I still don't know. What I do know is that my chosen lifestyle created a very specific dating pool and the water in it was murky and polluted. I was used to a certain type of man, and that type followed me into my recovery. Even down to the one-legged gangster, they were all alike in some way.

Ethan was no longer a safe option for me from the moment I suspected he was using. In retrospect, if I'd valued myself and my recovery more, I would have avoided romantic relationships completely during such an important season. But I was still just going through the motions. I still lacked the determination to truly save my own life, pressing forward only with the will to survive the next obstacle.

I wish I had some valuable insight on how to pick better partners, but I don't. I never learned. Instead, I've avoided romantic interests for most of my life since I got clean, being too traumatized or too fearful to let anyone close enough to change my opinion. In some ways, I wonder if I would even be able to maintain a relationship with a "regular" guy after the types of men I have chosen. Would I ever be able to live with "normal"? I do see beautiful relationships that exist for others, but for me, it's just never quite worked out. And that's okay. These days, I value myself enough to not be brought down by broken men anymore.

I have always struggled with identifying my emotions. Pregnancy and the bomb that Ethan dropped on me about his new romantic interest left me completely stumped again. Whether I was hurt, angry, sad—it didn't matter. I felt that I needed to keep any emotion tightly inside me to be able to navigate through this newest obstacle.

The mind is a powerful thing, protecting us from feelings that are too big or hard to process, and the only thing I could think to do was the next indicated step. I think that is a valuable lesson. It's better not to try and figure everything out at once, but to take one step at a time, allowing each step to lead us to the next.

REFLECTIVE QUESTIONS

1. Attraction goes beyond biology or chemistry, and we're often drawn to a certain "type" for a reason. How would you describe your attraction style? Can you identify why you're drawn to that kind of person?

_____

_____

_____

_____

2. Have you ever experienced something traumatic in a romantic relationship? If so, what happened and how did it affect you?

_____

_____

_____

_____

3. Emotions can be hard to name, especially if you've spent a lot of time chasing numbness. How well do you identify your emotions? What do you do when you're unsure of what you're feeling or why?

_____

_____

_____

_____

Chapter 12
Changing Course

"If you do not change direction, you may end up where you are headed."

~ Lao Tzu

I spent the next few days quiet, as I silently considered all the different places that my life could be headed. It was like the road ahead branched out in so many possible directions that I had to just stand still for a minute and take it all in. Ethan had been calling nonstop, and I'd been ignoring him. While I knew I would answer the phone eventually, I felt like I needed some time to process what he'd said to me the last time we spoke.

I knew I should have emotions about everything that was happening, but I felt numb. A blanket of nothingness sat heavily on me, reminding me that my desire to feel less pain throughout my life had, in turn, taken the rest of my feelings with it. I was pregnant, single, homeless, and facing potential prison time. I should have been scared—more scared than when I found out I was pregnant with Carter at nineteen. Instead, I felt nothing.

If it isn't obvious by now, I was never truly capable of taking care of my son, whether it was because of the drugs, my age, or the way my family stepped in so much that I never felt the need to try harder. The truth is,

I often felt like I was just watching from the sidelines while my mother and sisters raised him.

The first year of his life was spent in Las Vegas. My mom worked all day, and I stayed home with the baby. When she got home, I'd leave Carter with her and go run the streets, coming back by morning.

One day, the cops showed up at the door looking for me, to inquire about my involvement with a local crime. This finally changed the routine. My little sister, seventeen at the time, was home alone with the baby, and her having to deal with that on her own was the final straw for my mom. Her solution was to move us to California.

When we left, I had the best of intentions to do and be better—to get a real job and balance my time between work and single parenthood. But I had such a skewed sense of reality that I brought a giant bag of drugs with me, believing I would need them to be able to maintain long enough to get my life together once we were there.

At first, it went exactly according to plan. I was hired at a fancy hotel down the street, my mom and I would alternate work schedules, and as long as I had a little bump of the drugs throughout the day, I was able to function. Once that bag ran out though, everything changed. Trying to get clean at that point would have ruined everything. So instead, I hopped into an *AOL* chatroom and asked if anyone had what I was looking for. Surprisingly, a man responded.

At first, I would meet him down the street to pick up, but then he started inviting me to party with him at his house. Once I agreed to that and started meeting people with the same extracurricular activities as myself, my home life slowly started to drift further and further from my mind and my priorities. It became harder to get home in time for my mom to get to work, harder for me to make it to work at all, and harder for my son to be properly taken care of as he started walking, talking, and needing more constant attention.

My ignorance of my mother's needs caused us to fight a lot. When we fought, the baby would cry. I remember hearing him crying one day while my mother and I shouted and thinking to myself that I was destroying his young life. I could see that I was becoming someone that I hated, and if I didn't want my son to hate me, or worse, become me, I needed to get out.

When my older sister moved in to help, I basically moved out. I shifted into the nomad life of couch-surfing and gallivanting with all the new people I was meeting on the streets. My mother showed up to the motel room I was staying in one night to tell me that she'd gone to court to take guardianship of Carter. I didn't blame her for that. I knew what state I was in, and I would have signed anything to keep him safe from me. I truly believed that I was doing him a favor by not exposing him to the disaster that I had become.

What I did blame her for was not telling me about the court date in advance, which allowed the court to classify my son as abandoned when I didn't show up. While I was relieved that my son ended up with my mother and not anywhere else, I still felt deceived and betrayed.

My mother never kept Carter away from me. She allowed me to participate in whatever capacity I could manage from one week to the next. We would go to the movies or the park, or we'd be dropped off at Chuck E. Cheese, where we'd play skeeball and eat pizza until we ran out of money. As long as I was able to function, she never denied me time with him. She made sure that he knew I loved him and wanted to be with him, but that it was safer for him if I wasn't. When it was time for them to leave, I would buckle him into the backseat of the car and try not to cry. I understood that this broken family life was normal for him, but still wanted to protect him from feeling the same pain that I was.

When I started to receive jail sentences that grew longer every time, the months would pass by without much contact at all other than the postcards I would send him with cartoon drawings on them or the two-minute chats on the phone when I had enough commissary for a phone card. Once I was released, we'd go back to our weekend visits until the next incarceration, and the cycle would start all over.

Carter had struggles of his own. He received an ADHD diagnosis and displayed some emotional tendencies that mirrored tendencies of my own. He was in therapy for the majority of his childhood, trying to navigate through a scary world he never asked to be in. I think in some ways he understood that our family was different, but he was tough, resilient, and stronger than a child his age should ever have to be. He loved me in ways I had never been loved by another person, even though I didn't believe I deserved it.

So now, sitting on Skid Row, I analyzed my current situation, where I was expecting a second child. I knew that abortion was not an option for me, and that I would have to go to great lengths to have this outcome be different. I would have to let Ethan help me navigate my next steps, as I didn't want another fatherless child, tell the programs I was in that I was pregnant and ask them for help, and do whatever it took to make sure I did not repeat my same past mistakes with this new life growing in my belly.

By the time I told Sandra at the day program that I was pregnant, I only had two weeks left before I had successfully completed it. She responded with excitement about the baby and told me how the options that I had now could get me off Skid Row and into a shelter specifically designed for pregnant women. Since Ethan was still in Orange County, I asked her if we could start our search over there. Several options came up for possible places for me to go. We called two places that same day and made arrangements to visit and see if either would be a good fit for me.

The first place was a large house in the middle of a regular neighborhood. The walls were a light grey color that seemed to steal all the sunlight from the room. Here, I would pay the rent with my financial assistance, get a job whenever I could, and find another place to live within the first year after giving birth. There was nothing particularly memorable about this place, and nothing particularly wrong with it, I just didn't see it as anything other than another short-term solution.

The next place, Precious Life Shelter, was much larger, with a set of several homes on one lot. They were a sweet, pale yellow color with white trim and green plants, and the property had cute walkways surrounded by grass and flowers. Even though it looked so beautiful there, I struggled to see myself living anywhere that nice. It was such a stark contrast from where I'd spent the last five months. I was sure I'd never fit in. I didn't feel worthy of such a beautiful place after coming from somewhere so much dirtier.

Sandra and I met with the case manager, Wanda, and she showed me around and told me about their program. The first thirty days would be spent in emergency housing, where I would be given the resources to apply for financial aid, find a prenatal doctor, and begin a job search. After that, if I was able to find work within those first thirty days, I would move to the house next door, which was a Transitional Living. This house was larger, and was where I would spend the remainder of my pregnancy and the first three months after the baby was born before hopefully qualifying for a small apartment in the back for the SPE (Single Parent Efficiency) portion. I would be able to stay there with my child until they were two years old.

I asked Wanda if I could have a day to think about it, and while she looked surprised that I wanted time to consider my very slim options, she agreed. She stated that if I waited too long before deciding and missed my window, the open bed could be taken by someone else, and I would lose my opportunity.

"I think Precious Life is your best option. It was beautiful, and Wanda was so nice, and you can stay there for a long time. I would go there if I was you," Sandra said as we drove back to LA from Orange County.

"I don't know, it was almost too beautiful. Maybe I'd be better off at the other place. Plus you heard what she said. If I don't go soon I could miss the open bed, and I still have two weeks left before I complete your program."

"Oh, don't worry about that. You have worked really hard, and you've already successfully completed the program in my eyes. I'll get you your completion certificate for the judge a little early. If you want to go to Precious Life, pack up tonight and I'll take you tomorrow"

I called Wanda the next morning to make sure she still had an available bed. By that afternoon, I was loading my bags into Sandra's car, hugging Vee goodbye, and heading to Orange County, leaving Skid Row as quickly as I'd arrived.

Precious Life Shelter was a little intimidating at first. Busy women appeared in every open door, and pregnant bellies seemed to come around every corner. The intake process required all my bags to be inspected and all my electronics to be handed over, including my cell phone. When Wanda first asked me to turn in my phone, I gave her an old one with no minutes on it, without disclosing that I had a second phone in my pocket. I sat in the dining room and secretly texted my mom under the table.

My mother hadn't been all too thrilled to hear that I was leaving LA to move into a pregnancy shelter in the OC. I couldn't blame her. She was already raising one of my children, and I wasn't even six months clean yet, in no way ready to take care of a second child when I'd never been truly capable of caring for my first. But as I texted her that they wanted to keep my phone and switch us to landline calls only, with phone hours being scheduled in advance, she encouraged me to hand both phones over and not break the rules before I'd even made it all the way through the door. So, begrudgingly, I walked into the office and handed Wanda my working cell phone.

The rules there were strict, with little to no room for bending them. Curfews, chores, weekly check-ins, recovery meetings, on-site classes, therapy, and job-hunting were all spelled out on our weekly productivity sheet, where we had to track everything we did to stay busy and in compliance. The expectations were high, but the fact that the case managers and program director believed homeless, pregnant girls like us could meet them said a lot. They saw more potential in us than we saw in ourselves.

The house manager in the emergency portion of the shelter, Wendy, was firm but caring. She had short, dusty blonde curls and wire-rimmed glasses. She kept us on task with making sure we woke up and went to bed on time, made it down the stairs and to the classroom promptly each morning, and signed in and out whenever we'd leave for the day. Her and I hit it off right away. We'd stay at the dining table chatting long after we had cleaned the kitchen and the other girls had already excused themselves to go up to their rooms.

I checked into the shelter the day before my twenty-eighth birthday, and the next evening, Wendy and Wanda brought out a cake for me, with my name written on it in brightly-colored icing. I couldn't even remember the last time I'd seen my name embossed on a dessert in celebration.

The first thirty days flew by, with appointments filling the calendar that I had to find while riding a public bus in a town I'd never been to, without a cell phone for guidance. I also had to journey back to the courthouse for my three-month check in, where I was able to present the judge with a certificate of completion for the rehab and provide a letter showing that I was now living in a pregnancy shelter in Orange County. This time, he continued me on probation and set the next court date six months out instead of three.

Once that was done, all the rest of the appointments were taken care of; I applied for financial assistance and WIC, had a doctor lined up, and insurance. It was time to begin the job search. For me, this was the hardest part.

Pregnancy doesn't really lend itself to a job search, but I had to carry something else to an interview besides my secret baby. Every time I filled out an application, I had to face it: *Have you ever been convicted of a crime?*

Most people don't have to wonder if they should lie or not. But then, most people don't have to face the reality that a felony conviction doesn't exactly open any doors. They don't walk into an interview with a giant "F" stamped on their chest. Eventually I decided to check the yes box and write "willing to discuss" in the lines provided for more detail. I figured if I could get an interview, I'd have an easier time defending myself in person than writing down that I was a convicted drug trafficker, legally speaking, and would potentially need a two-year leave of absence to serve out a prison sentence if things didn't go my way with the court.

Besides, my work history was spotty at best. I had no real jobs to add to a resume in the past five years. I had to get creative, putting down small things I had done for money as work experience and coming up with clever explanations for why I was twenty-eight years old and had giant gaps between each period of employment listed. I came up with most of this in my mind, though, since I struggled to even land an interview at most of the places I applied.

As I left the shelter on the morning of my twenty-ninth day of job searching, I was feeling discouraged and nervous that I was on the brink of losing my place to stay. I had to get hired by the thirty-day cut-off as per the requirements of the shelter.

On a whim, I walked into a giant store that had holiday decorations from one end of the building to the other. It was the middle of October, and the mix between Halloween and Christmas decor was overwhelming, but I walked up to the counter and asked for an application. I brought it outside so I could fill it out and bring it right back in. When I carried it back in, I was surprised to be handing it directly to the hiring supervisor, who asked me several questions right on the spot about my availability and when I could start. I answered her and headed back to the shelter.

"How was the job search today?" Wanda asked as I entered the office to sign back in.

"I talked to the hiring manager at a store not too far from here, but that's it really. I'm starting to get nervous, I know I hit my thirty days tomorrow."

"We wanted to talk to you about that. We know you have some challenges working against you for employment, and we can see how hard you've been trying. We are going to extend you by fourteen days. Keep searching, God is going to bring you to the right place at the right time."

I thanked Wanda and headed into the emergency house for the night. The next morning, she found me right before I headed out for another day of job searching to give me a phone message that had come in the night before. I called the number back, and it was that same hiring manager I had spoken to at the holiday store, Stats, offering me a temporary seasonal position, set to start immediately. I guess I had walked into the right place at the right time after all.

REFLECT

Every new mother wonders if she is doing a good job or not. The responsibility we have to help mold a new life is massive, and when there's only one active parent, that responsibility doubles in size. Leaving Carter with my mom during those early years is something I spent years working through, so I could forgive myself for all that I missed out on and all that I put him through. It took a really long time for me to understand that I made the best decision for him at the time.

Caregivers will not always be as enthusiastic to keep a parent who is in active addiction present in the lives of their children as my mother was. She made exceptions for me, and while I didn't always agree with some of the choices she made for my son, I always stepped back and let her take the lead. I understood that she was the one with him day-in and day-out, and therefore she knew far better than I did what he needed.

Choosing the program that had higher expectations, more rules and restrictions, and what felt like unattainable standards was not ordinarily what I would have done. But spending almost six months in the shelter on Skid Row pushed me to want something better for myself. I knew somewhere inside that I would do whatever it took to not have to go back. We are resilient people, and we can do so much more than we realize when the stakes are high enough. Sometimes pressing into that hard task, showing up even when we're scared, and giving up the things we think we need in order to get something better creates a pivotal moment that leads to a greater change within us than we thought we were capable of.

Some of us have to work harder than others to find employment, whether we spent our younger years on drugs, never wanted to pursue higher education, or just don't know what we want to do with our lives yet to earn a living. We don't all have fancy degrees or specific talents that would open doors for us, and that can make the search for work tedious and challenging. We cannot let those details discourage us or hold us back. If we pound the pavement, show up with enthusiasm, and push some of those closed doors open for ourselves, we will always find what we need. It may not be glamorous at first, but it will always be better than doing nothing at all.

REFLECTIVE QUESTIONS

1. It's completely normal to question our parenting and wonder if we're getting it right. Describe a moment when you doubted yourself as a parent or caregiver. How did you work through that experience?

_____

_____

_____

_____

2. Describe a time when you gave up something comfortable to pursue something harder, but ultimately better, for your growth or future. How did it turn out, and what did you learn from the experience?

_____

_____

_____

_____

3. Money is a basic necessity, but earning it isn't always easy. Have you ever struggled to find steady work or income? What made that season difficult, and what has changed since then?

_____

_____

_____

_____

Chapter 13
Finding the Words

"Sometimes we motivate ourselves by thinking of what we want to become. Sometimes we motivate ourselves by thinking about who we don't ever want to be again."

~ Shane Niemeyer

Life at Precious Life Shelter was busy but good. After I had been there a few weeks, my mom brought Carter down to visit me. She'd brought him once to LA while I was living there, but having them see me in this new place, with nicer people around me, was so much better for all of us.

One afternoon, my little sister, grandmother, and the same aunt and uncle who had visited me on Skid Row came and took Carter and I out for our birthdays, which are two weeks apart.

This was the first time I'd seen my baby sister, Stevie, in a long time. She was polite and seemed genuinely happy to see me. She gave me a real hug and said how proud she was of me for the almost six months of dedication that I had managed to piece together so far. I could tell she had some concerns about how long I would last this time and obvious doubts about the pregnancy, as she seemed to keep a safe distance when she first arrived. But she didn't say any of that, and instead chose to show me kindness right away.

Stevie and I had a pretty typical sibling relationship growing up. One minute we were besties, and the next we were shouting and pulling each other's hair. We grew up to be super close in our teenage years, even though our lives couldn't have been more different. I, obviously, was the problem child, getting in trouble at school, bringing drugs and guys into the house and running the streets of Las Vegas until the sun came up. Stevie ran with the popular crowd, the quintessential home-coming queen who danced ballet well into college. We had our issues, but we were in it together to the bitter end.

There was a lot of insanity in our home growing up. Whether it was from our father's angry outbursts, our mother's propensity for gam-bling and avoidance, my mental health struggles, or the types of people I brought into the house. Criminal activity lurked around every corner in my life, so my sister was often exposed to things that forced her to grow up just as quickly as I did. Though for me, advanced maturity was a choice, for her, it was an undesired side effect of being related to me. She tried to keep a connection with me even well into the more chaotic times of my life, but she finally cut me off after I missed her college graduation because I was too strung out to get there. I'm not sure what made her give me another chance this time, but she quickly became my biggest cheerleader as I started working through this newest venture toward recovery.

My big sister, though, did not come back around as easily or as quickly.

For as long as I could remember, my older sister, Breana, lived in her own world. She beat her own drum, didn't rely on the approval of others, and was always very vocal about what she felt on any given topic, often delivering her opinions with hostility and bite. When we were little and our father would erupt into rage and destruction, she would don her older sister cap and distract us from the sounds coming from behind the closed door. But as we got older, we drifted further and further apart.

During our teenage years, after my mother finally packed us up and moved us out from our family home and into a small apartment, it was just me, mom and Stevie. Breana stayed with our dad and then left for college in Oregon. Our relationship was strained even more after we all left for California and she chose to stay in Las Vegas and remain living with our dad. She saw firsthand as his addictions worsened, and she became exposed to the truth of what a drug dependency truly looked like.

When things got too hard for her there, she joined my mother in California, moving in to help out with Carter as I was moving out. She voiced her opinion on the way I lived loudly and frequently and didn't coddle me when I'd try to get clean and fail or spend more and more time in jail. Some days it was as if I didn't have an older sister at all. Other days it was like I had a built-in savage truth-teller who would force me to see the reality of who I was when I preferred to live in my own shroud of denial.

She did, however, become a lighthouse for Carter, and the person he trusted and clung to. In many ways, she became the person he valued the most in this world. She always told him the truth, and I think he taught her about love after so many years where she struggled to feel it. It would still be a while before we reconnected, long enough for me to show that I was sticking to it this time and not planting a seed of false hope into my family once again. I didn't like that, but I respected it.

It felt good to have some of my family show up for me, even though none of them were all too thrilled about the circumstances of a new baby. It even felt good to get up and go to work everyday, move over to the Transitional House, and start building a routine.

Even though all these new pieces of my life seemed to be going in the right direction, I struggled to feel anything about the pregnancy. Every conversation with Ethan stung as he continued to share his feelings of excitement. He didn't feel like he had to change anything in his own life, while I was fighting to change everything. I could often tell when he'd been using and would cut those conversations short, attempting to ignore my pressing anxiety about what that situation would be like once our child was born.

The longer I was there, the more desperate I became to stay. I deeply understood that I was just one bad day away from ending up right back on Skid Row. I pushed myself to follow the rules, make it to my classes, and turn in my assignments. I shined when it came to avoiding drama amongst the other ladies when the pregnancy hormones in the house would all slam into each other and create shrill voices of argument throughout the hallways. I attended the weekly meetings as required, filled out check-in forms for my PO monthly, and stayed within the boundaries of the program, either from a true desire to change who I had always been or a sheer desperation to not be kicked out. It didn't matter the motivation. I just had to stay.

Eventually, myself and a group of young women in the house began to get along relatively well with each other. Friendships started to form amongst a few of us. We became a little crew of rough-around-the-edge ladies who were all coming out of a life full of challenges and obstacles. We could relate to each other's circumstances so well that a bond forming between us was inevitable. Even though we had different stories, different statuses with our baby daddies, and different reasons for ending up where we were, we still respected each other's struggle and willingness to change.

There were a few ladies that didn't land in our tight-knit group, one of which was an eighteen-year-old girl with a tendency to tell tall tales who latched on to me as her "big sister" in the house. She and I had arrived at the shelter in the same week, and our babies had the same due date. You could rarely tell if the stories she told were true or make-believe, but she'd had an interesting life for someone so young and seemingly so innocent.

Another woman came to the shelter pregnant with her sixth child, already having lost custody of the other five. Fresh out of an abusive relationship, she wasn't able to hold onto her children as she sought a new life for them. She had to leave them behind for a while as she exhausted the resources offered to her to get them back. Her goal was to eventually have all of her children under one roof with her. From my very limited vantage point, this seemed impossible, or at the very least improbable. To her, it was only a matter of time before it all worked out.

While the days were long and busy, they mostly passed by with ease. I adjusted to this new life—one that I didn't hate, or wish was different, or spend hours trying to numb myself from. I was able to take a little pride in my accomplishments. I felt encouraged by the staff, I laughed with my friends, and I was slowly learning how to function like a normal adult as I continued to work full time and make some connections at my job. The potential prison sentence was no longer front and center in my mind, threatening to steal my focus. Instead, it rested somewhere quietly in the back of my mind as I began to build hope that I might actually beat the case.

While all of this was good, I still struggled to feel any real connection to the life growing inside of me. I can't quite explain the disconnect, but something about this pregnancy felt so different from my pregnancy with Carter. Even as the weeks passed, I battled with the inability to bond maternally.

With Carter, I'd had a midwife and a home birth, but Precious Life didn't allow home births to happen inside their facility. So, I scheduled my check ups with an OB/GYN that worked at the hospital across the street, even though I had very little desire to give birth there. I participated in the fun "mom" events that the shelter held as the holidays approached and tried my best to anticipate balancing this new life with an infant.

Some days, though, I felt like I was holding on for dear life, white-knuckling every new challenge without the drug that had brought me peace for as long as I could remember. My mind would tell me that this was all temporary, and it was inevitable that I'd end up back in the throes of addiction. The likeliness of rearrest or falling into old habits seemed impossible to avoid. I had never been able to maintain a life as a regular, functioning member of society and had no faith in myself that I'd be able to do it this time either, baby or not. But I never felt like I could say any of that out loud, instead believing that I had to hold it all inside and keep a strong face as I went through the motions of recovery.

One of the requirements of the shelter for anyone with a drug addiction was to attend recovery meetings like Alcoholics Anonymous (AA) or Narcotics Anonymous (NA). While I have never considered myself to be an alcoholic, as drinking never really entered my mind as an alternative to the drugs I wanted, the closest meetings to the shelter was a Wednesday night AA meeting at the hospital across the street and a daily, early-morning AA meeting at the church two doors down. I was able to make the Wednesday meeting with ease, and our little friend group of girls walked over to the hospital together weekly to listen to the stories of the hardships and victories that the people of the program were experiencing. But I struggled to make it to the early morning meeting as I often needed to leave to walk to work before it had ended.

Because of this, Wanda firmly suggested that I participate in another program called Celebrate Recovery, a faith-based twelve-step program held at a church a few miles away. The leadership team there had volunteers who would pick us up every Friday night and transport us to and from the church. The meeting would count as two hours of productive time instead of one on our weekly sheet because it was longer, so I would get an extra hour of free time on my day off. Since I didn't have any other options, I agreed to go.

Walking in for the first time was intimidating. The church was huge, and the building we met in, with the word "warehouse" stamped on the outside wall in large letters, was packed full of people.

The meeting was split into two parts. The first half was spent listening to a speaker who would either share their testimony or a teaching, and the second half broke off into small groups. The other Precious Life girls and I found seats in the back and sat quietly for the teaching, then broke off to go find our small group. I realized at this point that not everyone in attendance was there for addictions or alcoholism. Some were there for anger, codependency, or relationship issues. There was a different group for each struggle, and we were allowed to attend whichever group we wanted. I went to the addiction group in hopes that I would try to fit in or, at the very least, *blend* in with the other addicts.

I attended the addiction group for a few weeks before I ever shared, listening to the other women talk about their struggles for a while as I built up the nerve to talk about my own. I'd spoken up a little in the outpatient program, since participation was part of their requirements, but hadn't done much talking outside of there. I spent my time in the AA meetings listening instead. It was hard for me to find the right words, especially now and especially here, at a church in a nice neighborhood with people who looked like their addictions hadn't taken them to the same dark places that mine had.

The story that finally got me to speak came from a bold, robust woman with warm, light skin that glowed as she spoke with passion and confidence. Her voice was loud, carrying with it a natural intensity that increased as she talked about her current place in life. She was a single mom living with her young son in a motel, trying desperately not to drink or get high, feeling like a failure but having the audacity to believe that this time, things could be different. I listened to her with my full attention and awe, until it dawned on me that if she could share these kinds of things, then so could I. When the time came for me to speak or to pass, I decided to try and find the words worth sharing.

"My name is Kelsey, and I'm an addict..."

REFLECT

The beginning stages of reconnecting with family after so much distance is different for everyone. Some of them come back with arms wide open, like the father welcoming home his prodigal son, offering love and support without question. Others will need a little more time to see for themselves that change is happening, and some will never come back at all. We can't blame anyone for how they choose to process our return, understanding that for some, it isn't always easy to forgive and forget. It's important to respect the time and the space that they need.

If you are the friend or family member of an addict, the best advice I can give is to lead with love, whatever that looks like for you. Sometimes that will require strict boundaries, allowing your loved one the space they need to see the direction their life is headed while protecting yourself at the same time. Sometimes that love is more sympathetic, offering a listening ear when they need to talk or helping them out if you see that they are truly trying to change. And sometimes that love is going to be found in releasing your loved one completely for a while, no matter how hard it may be to do so.

Building up the courage to finally speak up and share about what was happening in my life took me a long time. There is something freeing about having someone there to just listen, not to offer advice or give suggestions on how they would navigate through our lives. And being in a setting where everyone is struggling with something similar allows us to find the confidence in ourselves to open our mouths and talk. There are many things that we hold inside, thinking we are sparing those around us by not speaking up. But sometimes, the thing you are hesitant to share is exactly what the person sitting next to you needs to hear.

Whether you find that support at a recovery meeting, through a therapist, or through a close friend or confidant, it doesn't matter. The most important piece of the puzzle is in letting those thoughts that are trapped inside come out, so that they don't hold power over you anymore. Sometimes, it's our own minds that trap us, weaving invisible chains that hold us in place. The thoughts we fear, or the doubts we nurture, can become the loudest voices in our lives, convincing us that we're not enough, not capable, too broken, or not worth saving. There are times when the greatest battle we face isn't with the world around us, but it is fighting our own minds, where fears and insecurities rise up the loudest.

REFLECTIVE QUESTIONS

1. No family is perfect, and it's natural to feel disillusioned by this at times. Are there any estranged relationships in your family? What do you think has kept them from being mended?

_____

_____

_____

_____

2. Speaking up can be difficult but is often necessary for healing to begin. How comfortable are you with sharing your thoughts and feelings? Is there anything you can do to improve in that area?

_____

_____

_____

_____

3. Joining a support group can be intimidating, especially since the first step is often the hardest. Have you ever attended a support group like Celebrate Recovery? What was that experience like for you?

_____

_____

_____

_____

Chapter 14
Seeing the Light

"It is during our darkest moments that we must focus to see the light."

~ Aristotle Onassis

I woke up early with a bad feeling. I hadn't heard from Ethan in over a week, which was odd for him. Even though we weren't in a relationship anymore, he had still made it a habit to call the shelter every few days to check in. His sister had come by on one of my days off to pick me up and take me to hang out with the two of them for a few hours. He had even shown up in the back parking lot of the shelter a few times, just to say hello. I used the house phone that morning to call his cell and was surprised when his sister picked up.

"Oh, hey Kelsey. How are you doing?" she asked.

"I'm good. Busy. I haven't heard from Ethan in a while, and I wanted to check on him, make sure he's okay?"

"He's fine. He's in jail, but he's fine," she said jokingly.

"What! What happened?"

"I'm not really sure, but I don't think he'll be there that long. Maybe a few months? I'll make sure he calls you as soon as he's out, and if you need anything at all, please call me."

"I will, thanks." I said and hung up.

I wasn't sure how to process Ethan's latest visit to jail. I knew he had always had a rough relationship with freedom and struggled to stay out of trouble since he was young. I was pretty certain he'd been using again, but when I talked to him, it never seemed like he was up to no good. It made me realize how little I knew about his life beyond the surface, when I wasn't seeing him or talking with him daily.

With the holidays quickly approaching, my hours at work began to increase. The store was set to go out of business soon after the new year, so there were sales and discounts, and plenty of opportunity to gather some overtime hours along the way. I took advantage of any extra hours they offered as long as they didn't interfere with the requirements of Precious Life.

As I stood on my tiptoes on a ladder one day, hanging ornaments on hooks that were pegged into the panelled walls, I felt something in my lower abdomen that made me pause, climb down quickly, and head to the restroom. I wasn't sure what to expect as I went into the stall but didn't panic when I found that I was ever-so-slightly spotting blood. I was about twenty weeks along by this point, well past the timeframe when this should usually cause alarm, so I went back out to the sales floor and kept on working.

Seeing the blood did take me back a few years in my mind though, to another eerily similar moment.

I'd found out I was pregnant in a bathroom stall at a public park during one of the lowest points of my addiction. The father wasn't my boyfriend, he had a girlfriend already, and he'd just been arrested on warrants. It probably sounds like the exact same story I lived through with my son. And it was, just on repeat. A different man. A different girlfriend. A different baby. The same me.

I had never really learned the value of being in an honest relationship. I had been trained to be the other woman and trained well, from a young age. I made adulterers out of many men over the years and while I'm not proud of it, I think it's a testament to how the hardness around my heart continued to increase with each infidelity.

I was so far gone back then that I didn't even try to get clean after discovering I was pregnant. I was bouncing from one motel to the next, getting kicked out for either not paying on time or breaking the rules. I'd started seeing a new guy. He was wild, unpredictable, and always fully stocked with dope. No one around me ever suggested I slow down or get cleaned up for the pregnancy, so I didn't bother. It honestly didn't even occur to me.

I was maybe ten weeks along when the bleeding started. Somewhere inside, I knew what was happening. I called my mom and told her I needed help. She picked me up from the motel and drove me to an Urgent Care where the doctor confirmed that I was miscarrying.

I was too high to feel anything. Numb as always. But I still remember the way my mother quietly thanked God under her breath that the baby hadn't made it.

When we stepped outside, I asked her if she could drive me back to the motel.

"I have to get back to work. This has taken too long already," she said.

And she left.

So I walked—mid-miscarriage, dazed and bleeding—four miles back to the motel. And when I got there, it was the tweekers inside who offered me comfort and asked if I was okay. It was the people who should have been the most heartless who showed the most care.

I had kept my current pregnancy to myself at work, hiding it under loose, button-up shirts and steering clear of any conversation that might reveal the truth: that I was pregnant and living at the homeless shelter down the street. Only one coworker knew, and I went to her straight from the bathroom to ask her what I should do. Of course, she suggested I leave right then and head to the ER, but I was at ease. I wasn't in pain or bleeding badly, and I needed this job. I wasn't in a position to leave in the middle of their busiest season. Instead, I agreed to let her give me a ride to the hospital once my shift was over.

"Want me to stay with you?" she asked as we pulled up to the entrance of the emergency room.

"No, I'm sure it's fine. I live right down the street, and I'm almost five months along. It's probably nothing"

"Okay, well if you change your mind, call me and I'll come back. I hope everything is alright."

"I will. Thanks again for the ride," I said, climbing out of the passenger seat and walking through the doors.

I called the house manager at Precious Life from the waiting room to let her know where I was. The sky had already darkened, and curfew was approaching. The ER was quiet, and I sat there, unsure of what to do, watching the minute hand tick away on the black and white wall clock as I waited for them to finally call me back to a room.

The nurse took my vitals and said she would be taking me back for an ultrasound to check the status of the baby. I waited silently a little while longer until being escorted back to the ultrasound room. Because I'd had Carter at home instead of in a hospital, I'd only had one ultrasound with him throughout the entire pregnancy. I hadn't had any yet for this baby. But I had an idea of what the screen should look like.

"Go ahead and lie back for me and lift up your shirt. This might be cold," the technician said as she began to squeeze that clear liquid slime onto my stomach.

I did as she said and sat back as she used the wand to search my belly. Out of the corner of my eye, I could see the screen. The baby was still and seemed to float in the fluid that surrounded her. There was no motion, no kicking, just stillness.

"Is she dead?" I asked bluntly. I hadn't been told the gender yet, but at that moment I somehow knew that I'd been carrying a girl.

"I'm not able to share the results with you of what I'm seeing here. The doctor will have to explain everything to you," she said. But the way she looked at me and the change in her tone told me everything I needed to know.

She led me back to the ER waiting room with gentleness and compassion. I waited, alone and in silence, for the doctor to come tell me what I already knew. I thought that I should be feeling something in that moment but struggled to sense any emotion that could be lingering inside my core somewhere. I found nothing but silence.

When the doctor came in, he used the words *inviable pregnancy* and said I would need to go to my OB/GYN first thing in the morning to have a procedure to have the *fetus* removed. He said not to wait because my body could... he paused, then gestured with his hands, sweeping them down from the upper part of his stomach in a swift, swooping motion, never completing the sentence. His big words and hand gestures meant nothing to me, but I nodded and said I understood. He asked if I had anyone I could call, and I dialed the house manager at the shelter.

She expressed her condolences and asked if I wanted to be picked up from the hospital. It was almost 1:00am by then, and I didn't want to disturb anyone, so I declined and walked back to the shelter across the long parking lot and neighborhood streets. She was waiting for me at the door and gave me a hug, but I still felt nothing, totally numb to the emotion she seemed to be holding in.

The next morning, I went down to the office and was met by staff that had already heard the news. There was sympathy, and empathy, and love poured out all over me that I had no idea how to receive or react to. I called work to request a few days off for the medical procedure, and they lectured me for not telling them I was pregnant, saying they would have given me lighter work duty had they known. We ended the call with them giving me two full weeks off to recover.

The staff at the shelter had called one of their volunteers, Barbara, a sweet older woman with curly silver hair, to go with me to the doctor's office. Her skin looked pink in the cool winter air, and her voice was kind and gentle as she took my hand and promised to stay with me through the whole thing.

When we got to the office of the OB/GYN, though, we were met with bad news. The nurse at the front desk advised me that my government-issued insurance had changed, and I was no longer under the umbrella of the doctor I'd been seeing. He wouldn't be able to perform any procedure on me. She told me that the doctor next door would be able to assist instead. But when we got to the doctor's office next door, they told me I would not be able to make an appointment with them until I had my primary care physician provide a referral to his office.

I didn't have a primary care physician yet, I only had the OB/GYN that I was now unable to see. So, reluctantly, we headed back to the shelter to try and find a doctor that was in my new network who would be able to see me right away.

After several calls and most of the day slipping by, I finally managed to secure an appointment with a primary doctor about twenty minutes away for the following morning. I went to sleep for the second night with my *inviable* baby still in my womb. I still wasn't experiencing any cramping or discomfort, and the blood was a light trickle—nothing that caused much concern.

The next day, Barbara and I began by visiting the primary care doctor, who gave me the referral I needed. However, when I arrived at the new OB/GYN's office, I was told once again that he couldn't see me to perform the procedure due to his labor and delivery schedule. We set an appointment for the following morning for a D&C procedure, which is done to remove the fetus and check for any damaged tissue.

I spent these few days in a cloud of confusion. I struggled to process what was happening or how I could be left in this situation for multiple days because of something as futile as health insurance. I didn't know if this was normal procedure or not, and no one else seemed to know either. The shelter had never experienced a miscarriage as far along as I was, and so they trusted the medical professionals, just like I did. What choice did we have otherwise?

Deep into the third night, I woke up with horrible cramping. I tossed the blankets off my body to find blood that had been spilling out of me while I slept. I made my way into the bathroom of the shelter as my body went through the process to expel the lifeless little girl that I'd been carrying. In a state of complete shock, I sat still for a moment, with no idea what I should do next. The house was silent as everyone slept, but then I heard a voice—strong, and clear, and not my own.

"This is it. You can stay or you can go. But you have to choose," the voice said.

I didn't know what these words meant, or if I should be saying something in response. But in an instant, all of my fear, shock, pain, and horror evaporated, and I felt the presence of peace wash over me, holding me tightly. I felt a power that I'll never be able to accurately describe in human words pour love over me, covering me during a time of deep isolation and shame.

Somehow, I knew right then and there that God was real. He had chosen to speak to me. He had offered me a choice and filled me with comfort that didn't make any sense given my current situation, yet was deeper than anything I had ever felt before. God chose to reveal Himself to me and invited me to feel His presence physically and tangibly. His voice was filled with pure and unconditional love that turned pain into peace in an instant.

The silence of the night was broken by a crying baby on the other side of the house. One of the other residents walked into the bathroom holding her small, wailing child and said that when she woke up, she felt like God was telling her to come check on me. She looked around, taking in an understanding of what had happened, then handed me her daughter and ran down the stairs to get the house manager to help me.

It felt strange for a moment, holding a crying newborn so soon after my own loss. The weight of the tiny body in my arms, the warmth of her skin. It was a harsh contrast to the emptiness I had just experienced. But in that strange moment, it also felt ordained. As if God had purposely placed this living baby in my arms for me to comfort, just as He was offering His comfort to me. It was as if He was showing me that there was still life in the midst of loss, hope in the midst of devastation. It was a gentle reminder that even in the hardest times, there are new beginnings and fragile promises within the darkest moments. I could almost feel the weight of that promise. Life would keep going, and somehow, I would keep going with it.

REFLECT

I walked through tragic experiences throughout my life all alone because I was too stubborn to accept the help being offered to me by multiple people.

Asking for help, or even accepting it when it's offered, can be incredibly difficult. This is especially true if you've spent most of your life in survival mode, with experiences that have taught you that you can't rely on anyone else to take care of you the way you need. I struggled with believing that, as well as believing that my problems were small and insignificant, that I didn't deserve for anyone to go out of their way for me, and that I would always be better off handling everything all by myself.

These types of feelings are often rooted in pride. Even though, on the surface, it seems like I was putting others before myself, deep inside I didn't believe anyone truly wanted to or was capable of caring for me in the same way that I could care for myself.

Most of the time, if someone is offering to help you, they really do want to be there for you. It's okay to let your guard down once in a while and accept that help. It's not a handout, and it's not because they feel sorry for you. In most cases, I choose to believe that people really do want to be good to each other. I am still not great at accepting help, but I do see the value in one sister or brother helping another. Life can be challenging, and we were never expected to carry the burdens of this world all alone.

Experiencing a horrible loss can sometimes lead us to overwhelming emotion, but not always. For me, the feelings of numbness may have been a protective measure, may have been from the shock of it all, or I may have just not been capable of feeling anything in that moment. Instead of thinking that we are "supposed" to have any specific reaction to an event, I hope we are able to accept our emotions for what they are and not try to force ourselves to feel something that just isn't there.

Go easy on yourself if you're not always feeling everything the way you think you should.

Processing through such a heavy loss takes time. It will sometimes not happen until years after the event itself, when you can finally look at it with open eyes and accept that such a tragic experience took place. The way we respond to trauma or tragedy is often a gut reaction—a moment where an instinctual response is all we have to offer.

As the years have passed, I've learned that hearing from God audibly doesn't happen for everyone. In fact many people spend years trying to hear the voice of God. I have spent years praying to hear it again, and I believe I have, many times actually. But never in the same way that I heard it that first night. God's voice lives somewhere deep inside of us, and we have to practice silence and focus to be able to hear it. But I do believe that His voice is a free gift that we can access at any time, if we are willing to stay quiet for a minute and listen.

REFLECTIVE QUESTIONS

1. Asking for help can be challenging, and accepting it when offered can be just as tough. How comfortable are you with accepting help from others? Is this something you'd like to improve?

_____

_____

_____

_____

2. Burying painful emotions is something many of us do, but it's not always healthy. Are there any emotions you tend to avoid expressing? What are they, and why do you think you'd prefer to hide them?

_____

_____

_____

_____

3. God speaks to us in many ways. How do you recognize God's voice in your life? What does it feel or sound like to you?

_____

_____

_____

_____

Chapter 15
Staying Home

"The ache for home lives in all of us,
the safe place where we can go as we are and not be questioned."

~ Maya Angelou

After the miscarriage, I spent the next few days in my bed. I sat alone on the upstairs level of the transitional portion of the homeless shelter, while the other ladies continued with their daily lives of chores, tasks, and requirements. This left me with a lot of quiet time to contemplate what life would be like now that I was no longer pregnant. Eventually though, all that quiet contemplation turned into an emotional overload, and all I could do was cry.

I had the insight to realize that much of this emotional upheaval was hormonal, but that didn't mean that the sadness wasn't also real. However, the emotion I struggled to accept—couldn't even put words to at the time—was relief. There was an ever-so-small piece of me that felt relieved that I wasn't having a child with another incarcerated man, with no help from my family and little to no support outside of the shelter. Don't get me wrong, I was heartbroken to have lost the baby, but the reality of the situation was not missed by me. I knew how hard it would have been to raise this child alone in the current season of my life.

Wanda would come up and check on me every few hours, sitting on the edge of the bed and asking if I needed anything. Every time she walked in the room, I would cry some more. She was always gentle, supportive, and kind. She brought up sweet treats even though food wasn't allowed upstairs and offered me unconditional love and comfort. On the fourth day, she suggested I get up and come downstairs for a while, and I did.

"There is a group of women from the Celebrate Recovery group you've been attending coming tonight to have dinner with you all. Would you like me to let them know your situation before they get here, so they don't ask too many questions?" she asked, as we sat in her office at our first case management meeting since the miscarriage.

"Yes, I think that would be good."

"Okay, that's not a problem. I know you have another week off, but you can't spend the whole time upstairs in that room. How about volunteering over at the thrift store a couple hours a day until you go back to work?" she asked.

"That sounds fine," I said. The thrift store was located on the shelter's property, and it was run by volunteers to help raise funds for the facility's additional needs, ensuring it could operate without financial strain.

"Is there anything you want to talk about today?"

"Well, I am wondering what happens now. I'm not pregnant, and I don't have a baby so, what should I be doing?" I asked.

"The staff has already decided that you be allowed to stay for the same two months that we give to all residents after their child is born if they aren't approved for the Single Parent apartments upstairs. We won't require you to attend any of the parenting classes, but we will have to find other ways to fill your productive time. I'm sure it might be hard to be around all the other moms and babies, so you're welcome to leave earlier if you'd like. But we are not kicking you out. You have time. This was not your fault."

Outwardly, I hadn't considered the loss of the baby as my fault. But, somewhere in the deep trenches of my mind, I wondered if it was because of the damage I'd done to my body with drugs, the extra hours I was taking at work, or the lack of feelings I'd had for her that kept her from being able to grow. I didn't say any of that though.

"I know."

"We have resource lists with names and numbers for sober living homes, if you'd like to stay local. We can also get you access to a list for LA County if you'd like that instead, just let us know what you need."

"Thank you. For now, I think I'll keep working and collect as much money as I can before the store closes and I have to leave."

"I think that's a good plan. Now tell me, how are you doing with the loss?" she asked tenderly.

"I'm okay, I think. I do have waves of sadness, but I wonder how much of that is just my hormones being out of whack."

"It's okay to be sad, Kelsey. And it's okay to honor the baby who brought you here. You've done so well since you arrived. She gave you a new start! Let's find ways to celebrate her. Did you have a name picked out?"

"Yes, her name was Kylie. Kylie Elizabeth. I think honoring her is a sweet idea. I don't really know how to do that, but thanks for the suggestion," I said, wrapping up the conversation.

Later that evening, a group of four women showed up to the shelter. I waited a bit before heading downstairs, allowing them time to ooh and aah over the tiny babies before I came down and shattered the excitement. I anticipated pity and sympathy that I didn't really want.

I recognized the ladies from the Celebrate Recovery (CR) meetings but didn't know their names or anything about them. Surprisingly, none of them expressed any pity. They gave out hugs and let me stay quiet as they told us that they didn't bring any food, but thought it would be more fun to take us all out to eat instead.

One by one, we piled into the backseats of their cars, squished amongst car seats and pregnant bellies. The driver started to ask us a few questions, but my attention was on the book that was partially sticking out of the little pouch sewn into the back of the driver's seat. The title read *Heaven is For Real: A Little Boy's Astounding Story of His Trip to Heaven and Back.* I pulled the book out and opened it up to a random page in the middle and started reading.

In the part that I read, the little boy, Colton, was talking to his mother about his trip to heaven. He told her that he'd met his little sister while he was there—the one who had "died in mommy's tummy." Colton had no way of knowing about the baby his mother had lost, but this knowledge, that her little baby girl was in heaven, comforted her and brought her to tears.

I thought about the voice I heard in the bathroom that night and wondered if this book being placed here for me to find, and this page that I had randomly opened to, might have been another message from God. I hadn't told anyone about the voice I'd heard for fear I would sound absolutely nuts or that it would be discredited because of the circumstances surrounding me at that moment.

"Have you read that?" the driver asked, looking at me in the rear view mirror.

"No, it just caught my attention. Do you think he really went to heaven?"

"I do, yeah. You can take that book if you want. I've already read it."

"Okay, I think I will, thanks." I said.

The CR lady I sat with at dinner that night was a spunky blonde with a giant pink flower clipped into the back of her hair named Irene. She cracked jokes about the streets and her old party days and made all of us shelter girls feel comfortable. She talked bluntly, dipping her tortilla chips into salsa as she chatted and laughed at her own dismal history.

"Wanda told us about the miscarriage. How are you holding up?" she asked, directing her attention toward me.

"I'm okay, I guess. Just trying to figure out what happens next."

"I know it must really suck, and it's not what you were expecting. But you know what? Sometimes life just sucks. I have a feeling you've walked through some pretty tough stuff already, am I right?"

"Yes," I said in agreement.

"And you're still here to tell the tale. That's what we do—we keep showing up. Even when we don't know why life is the way it is some days, we still show up and keep walking forward." Her directness was refreshing after interacting with so many people who preferred to tiptoe around the conversation or ignore it entirely.

A few days later, Irene was the speaker at the CR. Her testimony was raw, filled with drugs, mayhem, tragedy, and loss. For the first time, I listened to a story that I wholly related to, and that made me feel like maybe my own history wasn't as random and unique and unrelatable in this program as I'd originally believed. I walked right up to her afterwards in the church warehouse parking lot and asked if she would be my recovery sponsor. Without missing a beat, she said yes.

Irene and I hit it off really well, and she showed up for me over and over to help in whatever area I needed. She would bring me homework every couple of weeks to guide me through the twelve steps and would meet with me to go over the pages I'd written as I completed them. I found that I was able to be more honest with her than with anyone ever before, and she also shared stories with me that related to what I had done or experienced. She made me feel less alone in my isolated world of chaos and eagerly participated as my journey to healing finally began.

A few short weeks after I returned to work at Stats in early January, the store closed down as expected. I was once again without a job. I spent a lot of time volunteering at the thrift store and hit the pavement again, looking for the next door to open. Irene, a retired restaurant manager, had friends in that industry and offered to see if she could get me an interview at a diner across town. It wouldn't be the shortest commute, but there would be cash tips and one bus that would take me directly there. Waitressing hadn't ever been a consideration of mine, but I didn't have the privilege of being picky.

We sat down with the manager of the diner and chatted for a bit before he took me to a separate table for the interview. He asked me the standard questions, avoided some of the more personal topics—I assume because Irene had already filled him in on some of the details—and then abruptly asked me about my smile.

"Waitressing is part of the hospitality business. Our main focus is on bringing a smile to our customers, and it doesn't hurt your tips either. I noticed you haven't really smiled during our conversation. I'm just wondering why not?" he said.

"I don't have the best teeth. I prefer to smile with my mouth closed. That's all."

As stereotypical as it seems, the idea that drug abusers destroy their teeth is actually completely valid, or at least it was for me. I hadn't been to a real dentist since I was a teen, when he stopped mid-procedure and asked if I was going to tell my mom I'd been smoking meth or if he should. He explained that it left a residue on the teeth that he could see during the cleaning.

Obviously dentistry, and sometimes even a toothbrush, was a luxury I could not afford during my six years of homelessness. The only time my mouth would be inspected at all was in the county jail, where the doctors would handle toothaches with full-blown extractions instead of root canals or cavity fillings. I had some teeth missing from the back, and one closer to the front had been removed during my last stay, making my real smile a thing of the past for me. The shame I felt about having bad teeth caused me to shy away from many things, and smiling at customers in a diner was right up there on that list. I preferred to keep the holes in my mouth hidden.

"Look, I want to hire you, but you have to be able to smile. A real smile. If you worked here, do you think you'd be able to get over your insecurity and smile at my customers?" the diner manager asked.

"Honestly, no I don't. I'm sorry. Maybe this isn't the best job for me."

We shook hands, and I walked out the door to Irene's car, knowing I may have just let vanity create a missed opportunity. This wasn't the only part of my body that wore permanent markings from my past. Old images forever engraved on my skin in ink also covered me, leaving reminders that I could change as much as I wanted to on the inside, but the outside would always bear evidence of the life I used to live. I could hide many things about who I once was, but there are always remnants in the physical. The damage is sometimes easy to see and sometimes hidden away, but I will always know the story behind the scar, the mark, or the tattoo.

I finally ended up being hired by a man who owned three Subway restaurants in the area, alternating my shifts between each one. It wasn't a lavish job by any means, but the boss didn't care if I smiled with my teeth or not, as long as the sandwich was made.

I was twenty-eight years old with two teenage supervisors. One of them was sweet and fun to work with, and the other would show up a half hour late every day, flying into the parking lot on her motorcycle and hiding in the freezer for hours while we handled the lunch rush. She even offered me a line of cocaine once.

I knew the arrival of the date for me to leave Precious Life was inevitable. As it got closer, Irene would come take me to check out sober living homes in Orange County. I had only momentarily considered going to find a place closer to where my son lived. I knew that the closer I got to my old life, the harder it would be to stay on the right path. Instead, I decided to try and stay put where I was, since so far I had been doing pretty well at not falling back into old habits.

Every sober living home we checked out was a miss. The residents were often obviously not clean, there were very little requirements to stay there, and at some, there weren't even house managers or people to check in with. Irene thought it would be dangerous for me to live in any of them and, compared to Precious Life, nowhere that we visited seemed good enough.

"Why don't you come live at my house? You can sleep on the couch for a little while, and I'll clean out my spare room for you. I just don't think any of the places we've looked at are a good fit." She brought this up one day as we drove back to Precious Life from another day of touring sober living homes.

"You don't feel like that's going backwards a little? I just stopped couch surfing less than a year ago," I replied light heartedly.

"I don't think so. I think it's better than any of those other places we looked at. And we get along really well. I think it would be fun."

"Well, okay then. I guess I'm moving in."

The next day, I went into the office to tell Wanda the plan. I was excited and nervous about this change, knowing I'd probably have to quit the Subway job and start looking again closer to where Irene lived. But I was relieved to have a plan for where I was going.

When I sat down across the desk from Wanda, I eagerly started telling her that I thought this was a good idea and even though I didn't want to live on someone's couch ever again, the alternatives didn't seem like they fit for me. I had come too far to put myself back in such an uncertain situation.

Wanda listened politely, then paused when I finished. When she started speaking again, there was a subtle excitement in her voice.

"Kelsey, the staff and the board of directors want to offer you another option. You see along this back edge of the property, those apartments?" she asked, pointing toward the buildings to the left through the window. Those units, as far as I knew, were meant for reunification—for moms to have any of the kids they were separated from join them on the property once they were ready. They'd been empty since I'd arrived.

"Our plan is to offer extended living, a permanent residence, to those who complete the Single Parent Efficiency portion of the program. After the babies are two years old, the family would have the option to stay with no time limit. We have four units and no occupants. We would like to offer you a place there, as our first permanent resident. You can be our guinea pig!"

I was stunned, speechless, and not sure what to say. I just had a plan all ready to go. Irene was supposed to come get me and take me home with her. I needed a minute to consider the offer.

"Wow, Wanda, that's amazing, and I'm so honored you guys would think of me. But can I let you know in the morning? I need to think about this," I said.

Wanda, once again surprised that I wanted to take a moment of consideration regarding an incredible opportunity, rolled back in her seat and said simply "Yes, of course."

With a smile and a wave of her hand, she indicated that I was free to go.

I walked back over to the Transitional House and sat on the couch for a few minutes, chewing on the two options set before me. Suddenly, I thought of the words I had heard in the bathroom that night: "You can stay or you can go, but you have to choose." In an instant, it dawned on me that maybe *this* was that choice—this moment, and this place. And I knew what I had to do. I stood back up and ran back to the office.

When I walked in, Theresa, the program director, was in Wanda's office. I had watched Theresa from a distance since my arrival. She always seemed to float through the day with confidence and strength, not usually working hands-on with us girls but always treating us with respect and kindness. Many times, I had found myself looking up to her, hoping I could be like that one day: self-assured, positive, certain of who I was and what my calling was in this world. She wore her purpose well, and we could all see that she was fulfilling the call of her life.

"Kelsey, did you forget something?" Wanda asked as I barged in.

"Yes, I forgot to say yes. I don't know what I was thinking, of course I would rather stay here!"

"That's great news, Kelsey. Wanda, can Kelsey and I have a few moments in your office?" Theresa asked.

Wanda nodded and left. Theresa walked over to her side of the desk to sit. She pulled papers out of a manilla file folder, the words Lease Agreement written at the top.

"Kelsey, we were all ready to let you leave, but God just kept tugging at me, saying that you are supposed to be here. He wants so much more for you, and you have done so incredibly well. Even with all the odds stacked against you and all the challenges you've had to work through, you have persevered.

"This agreement will take you out of the program and make you a renter instead. You'll still have a curfew, budget classes, and a few other requirements, but we want you to be our very first permanent resident. I want to take the little 'h' out of your homelessness and put the big 'H' in your home. So, do you want to stay?" she asked.

"Yes, I'm staying! Where do I sign?"

REFLECT

Some of the most awful things we will experience in this lifetime will be no one's fault. How we accept these experiences without having anyone to blame will teach us a lot about ourselves and how we view the world. Not everything requires us to find fault in order to process through it, although our human nature often persuades us to believe otherwise. To quote my dear friend Irene, sometimes life just sucks. It's how we navigate through those difficult times that builds character and resilience.

Meeting someone like Irene was huge for me. I had spent so many years feeling like the way I had lived was too far outside the realm of "normal" to ever meet anyone who had actually made it out. I can see how that seems self-deprecating, but living in a world of such deep isolation, it was hard to imagine that anyone could relate to what I had done or been through. And getting out of the life actually is very rare, with statistics as low as 12% of addicts finding long term recovery without some type of support system in place. To meet someone with a life like mine with multiple years of clean time was exceptional and exactly what I needed.

Places like sober living homes often exist as an in-between stage; somewhere between a strict, inpatient program and normal day-to-day life. But they are not all the same. There are more important factors to look into than cheap rent and room size. If you are genuinely trying to stay on the right track, evaluating the safety of the home, how they handle conflict and relapse, and who is keeping the residents accountable is a good place to start. The last thing we want is for someone in active addiction to occupy the bed right next to you when you are in early recovery. Protecting yourselves from triggers and relapse starts from day one.

Being able to identify when an incredible opportunity is presenting itself, and walk through an open door without hesitation, requires us to be quick on our feet. Opportunities are missed every single day by people like me—someone who feels the need to evaluate every piece of information presented before committing. The more time I spent clean, the more fearful I became of making the wrong decision, terrified that I would end up back where I started. But God planted a tiny little seed of faith in me, showing me what I was supposed to do at that moment. Perhaps His words in the shelter that night had a much bigger meaning than this decision to stay at Precious Life, or maybe not, but remembering those words was what helped me make that quick decision to stay. Learning to hear His voice and trust what it says will always guide us through the important choices in our lives.

REFLECTIVE QUESTIONS

1. It's natural to want to find someone or something to blame during tough seasons, but that doesn't always help us move forward. In which areas of your life do you find yourself seeking blame? Do you tend to blame yourself more, or others?

    _____

    _____

    _____

    _____

2. Who do you look up to in your life, and what is it about them that you admire or wish to emulate?

    _____

    _____

    _____

    _____

3. Missed opportunities happen every day, often without us even realizing it. Can you describe an opportunity in your life that you
   missed? What held you back from pursuing it?

   _____

   _____

   _____

   _____

Chapter 16
Letting Go of the Past

"Some of us think holding on makes us strong,
but sometimes it is letting go."

~ Herman Hesse

As I moved into my own small apartment, I was quickly met with a newfound humility: I had no idea how to be an adult. I had to ask for help with even the most mundane of tasks. Wendy, the house manager of the emergency portion of the program, took me to the grocery store and showed me how to shop. Wanda had to take extra time to show me how to clean certain areas or remind me to clean at all, as I'd often let the clothes pile up and the dust cover shelves and tables with little to no thought. I had no idea how to pay a bill, or open a bank account, or follow a budget. The shelter began to teach me all of that with no judgment at all, gently guiding me into normalcy.

I found myself becoming more and more involved with members of Celebrate Recovery as Irene brought me to after-church lunches and events. I made friends with other ladies from the addiction open-share group and started to build myself a little community of people. We supported each other, and I was learning how to be in worthwhile friendships that weren't based in transactions but formed through community. It was nice to have friends, to be invited to things, and to be welcomed into places I had spent my whole life avoiding. The church,

SeaCoast Grace, was full of people that were kind to me, treated me with respect, and offered me a chance to be a part of a new kind of family.

When a baptism was offered at CR, I somehow knew that this was the next step for me. I didn't know exactly what it meant or why I needed to do it, I just knew that I did.

I stood on a stage and said a few words before being completely immersed in the water. I instinctively understood that this gesture symbolized my chance to have all that filth, shame, and disgust washed off of me so that I could start fresh as someone brand new. I had spent years wishing I could just start over. I never felt like it was possible to be fully forgiven for all that I had done, but Jesus gave me that chance—to wash away my old life and step into a brand new one. After the baptism, I prayed a simple prayer, but I meant it with everything inside of me.

"Okay, God, I'm here, and I want to try to do this life with you. But I need you to show me how to do all this. I can't do it by myself. Amen."

After that prayer, God showed up and honestly, He kind of showed off. I had so many challenges stacked up against me, and it felt like all I had to do was sit back and let Him lead the way as, one by one, He knocked down wall after wall and showed me that I could trust Him with my life and my circumstances.

I could see my prayer being answered in all kinds of different ways. I had a giant pile of debt with the county, so big that my driver's license had been suspended for years. When I called to set up a payment plan so that I could get my driving privileges back, the office told me that my case had been closed and that I owed nothing. They released the hold on my license, and I was at the DMV a few days later. Just a few days after that, someone donated an old car to the shelter, and Theresa gave it to me, saying that a car showing up days after I'd gotten my license back could only mean that God had sent it there for me. I struggled to believe that God cared about things like transportation and debt, but it was bigger than that. It was a chance to see a power working in my life that helped me step into a deeper understanding of what faith looks like.

A friend I'd met through CR brought me to a dentist for the first time in years. After miscarrying the baby, my teeth seemed to be getting worse and worse, and I was in a lot of pain. I was terrified walking in there, having to show my teeth to someone and not know if I'd be judged or if she'd even be able to help me at all. Not to mention the inevitable cost to repair the mess my mouth had become after abusing meth and wreaking havoc on my teeth.

But the dentist was so kind, understanding, and gentle with me. She offered to fix my teeth for a fraction of the price. She also explained to me that babies often take the majority of the nutrients from the mother during pregnancy, and since mine was struggling to stay alive in the womb, she must have been pulling as many nutrients as she could, resulting in the accelerated damage to my already-damaged teeth.

The long, intense journey of fixing my teeth was made longer and more intense by being in recovery. I did the whole process with nothing but tylenol and novacaine. Some days, it felt like the worst decision I had ever made. I sat in that chair with my mouth stuck open for hours at a time, followed by days of swelling and pain. But by the time the process was over, I realized just how valuable the outcome of this journey was. I hadn't realized how much my broken teeth had held me back until I could really smile again.

Theresa reinstated my cell phone privileges, and the move upstairs meant I got social media back too. I posted about my new apartment on Facebook, and my old supervisor from the holiday store saw it and commented. As it turned out, the staff at the local store had all shifted over to the location in Redondo Beach. They ended up hiring me as a part-time cashier. So, for a while I worked at both the Subway and the Stats Holiday Store.

My supervisors and coworkers at Stats became like family to me. One of the product designers was a pastor's wife, and she walked with me through the first years of my faith, patiently answering my questions and explaining things to me on a much deeper level than church on Sunday could. I saw God's hand in that too, the way that He placed me with someone who would walk through those early days with me in love and acceptance.

Ethan did eventually get out of jail and called me to check in. It wasn't easy telling him that I had lost our baby. Especially because he didn't believe me. He said that I was too far along for a miscarriage and accused me of trying to keep his child from him. He ended up showing up at the shelter to see for himself, and I watched him step back in surprise when I met him outside without the giant pregnant belly that he had expected to see.

Ethan and I stayed in touch for a while even after the loss though. Eventually, he ended up back out on the streets and then back in prison, facing an eighteen-year sentence. His family and I remained in contact the whole time, and I talked to him through calls and letters for the majority of the ten years that he was actually incarcerated. But after his release, he ended up right where he had always been when we'd met all those years before. Once he was back in active addiction, we spoke less and less, until we eventually stopped speaking entirely.

The young lady at Precious Life that I'd shared a due date with didn't have any local family, and her baby's arrival was right around the corner. She asked if I would step in as her birth coach and be in the room with her during her delivery. Although the shelter told me I didn't have to say yes, knowing it could be painful to be present for a birth at the same time that I should have been preparing for my own, I agreed to be there for her.

Witnessing a life coming into the world from the other side was such an incredible experience. Seeing the first breath and the first cry, cutting the umbilical cord, was like nothing I'd done before. I think there was healing in that too, another gentle reminder to not fall into bitterness or self-pity due to my own loss. These feelings were replaced with the awe and wonder that comes from the gift of life. She even gave her baby girl my middle name.

On April 7th 2012, I celebrated my first year in recovery after fifteen years of active addiction. It was the longest I'd been able to stay clean since I was thirteen years old. I know that first year had been bumpy, and I didn't do any of it perfectly, often gripping tightly to whatever and whoever I could find, knuckles white and aching through momentary lapses, bad decisions, and unexpected successes. But April 7th was the day I walked into that last rehab for the very first time—the day I chose to save my own life after so many years of barely scraping by, surviving by the grace of God alone, even before I believed in Him.

Six months after that, I walked into the courtroom for what would be the very last time as I unexpectedly received my final sentencing from the judge. I had brought all the usual documentation that I needed: letters from Precious Life Shelter, my sponsor, and the Celebrate Recovery program. I showed him that I was working two jobs, at the Subway down the street and the holiday store. The judge expressed his condolences after hearing of my miscarriage but was impressed to see that even despite the loss, the pregnancy shelter had offered me a place to live anyway. Then he said something I never expected to hear.

"Miss Harris, it's been a *long* road, and you have walked it well. Despite the challenges presented before you, we have seen you show up for yourself, follow direction, and subsequently change your entire life.

This court and myself are *proud* of you for all the hard work you have done to change your circumstances."

He paused, momentarily directing his attention to the inmates behind the wire fence. "This young lady is an example to you all that change is possible, and that you can start over and do the right thing. Don't ever count yourself out, because she has shown us that it can be done and today, she has renewed my hope in the success of rehabilitation.

"I am pleased to formally *dismiss all* charges against you, Miss Harris, and continue you on probation. You are free to go, with no charges pending. I wish you health and happiness, and continued success in whatever you do from here."

After two long years, it was finally over. I walked out of that courtroom with my head held high. I felt surprised at what the judge had said and proud of myself that I had finally done something right within the court system, a feat I had never expected to accomplish.

But the biggest miracle was the way my desire to get high disappeared. The moment I surrendered to God, it was like all the urges to use, the desperation for numbness, the deep longing for what I once desired over anything else in this world—it just left. Just like that. It was almost as if all the years of addiction were washed away in the water of baptism, leaving no residue of it at all. At first, I didn't even realize that it was gone, but I slowly began to notice that I didn't feel like an addict anymore. I felt like I had finally let it all go. I felt healed.

I knew that I should feel grateful for having the weight of my addiction and the threat of a prison sentence lifted from my shoulders. But my path forward was still such a mystery to me. Who was I going to be, if I wasn't a meth user or criminal? Who did God want me to become? Despite my nervousness about the future, I was glad to feel a subtle sense of happiness and optimism replace the numbness I had felt for so long. Maybe I could discover a higher purpose after all.

REFLECT

Having to ask for help for seemingly small tasks was hard for me at first. It was a little embarrassing to be nearly thirty years old and not know how to do normal day-to-day things, but there was no shame in it at all. My life had looked very different from the average adult. When you are forced into survival mode, there are more important things to worry about than how to find the cheapest item in a grocery store aisle or not leave the debit card in the ATM machine when you walk away (I did that at least four times). The lesson here is that there is no "normal" to life. We are all on individual paths, and over the years, I have learned that there are many things that I do know how to do that others do not. Street smarts are still smarts, and they come in handy more often than you may realize.

Baptism and prayer were crucial for me to form a relationship with my Higher Power. God is so powerful, and He wants us to come to him, to be cleansed of all that dirt and grime we carry around, and be led by Him. There is humility in admitting that some days the piles are too high, the tasks are too hard, and the journey is too bumpy to be walked all on our own. When we lay it all at His feet, He can knock down those barriers and guide us to a rest that only He can provide.

It requires trust to do this, and after a while of seeing Him come through for me over and over, I finally started to understand what all those people who had told me to "just have faith" were talking about. It means giving it to Him and waiting with humble expectation for His solution, without trying to figure it all out on our own. In a lot of ways I am still learning to do this, but I get better at letting go all the time.

Addiction destroys much more than we realize. The damage I did to my teeth was an obvious destruction—one that anyone could see with their own eyes. But the damage that drugs have on the mind, the spirit, and the soul is just as real. An addiction to porn or sexual promiscuity can damage a marriage or future partnership. An addiction to gambling or shopping damages finances and credit scores. Being addicted to food can damage the body, causing obesity and illness. Anything that becomes an idol in our lives carries a risk with it. Too much of a seemingly good thing almost always ends in destruction.

Even things that we are not addicted to but that we keep around *just because* can serve little to no purpose. Alcohol was never a part of my addiction or personal struggle, so I've never really included it when counting my clean time. I could always take it or leave it, and while I understood that many people in recovery choose to group all things together, I didn't always see it that way. Over time, as God continued to work on me and challenge the way I thought or believed, I came to the conclusion that if I could leave it, I might as well. If there are seemingly small things in our lives that do not serve us, sometimes we can make an evaluation and decide to release them.

Life often presents us with full circle moments. Opportunities to see something to completion and then honor the time that we spent within the journey itself. We don't always get to see where we are headed while we are in the midst of the struggle, but once we've reached our destination, we can look back on the journey. And I think we can see why God took us on the route that He did. There are so many things we can't fully understand while we are sitting in the thick of it, but I promise it will all make sense eventually.

REFLECTIVE QUESTIONS

1. "Normal" is more of a state of mind than a standard to aspire to. What tasks that others might consider "normal" do you find difficult to get done? Who could you ask for help with them?

_____

_____

_____

_____

2. Baptism is often seen as a powerful symbol of leaving the past behind and stepping into a new life, free from the weight of old burdens. Have you ever been baptized? If so, how did you feel as you came out of the water?

_____

_____

_____

_____

3. Praise from an authority figure can be incredibly encouraging and motivating. Can you describe a time when someone in a position of authority praised you? How did it make you feel?

_____

_____

_____

_____

Chapter 17
Feeling Again

"The storm isn't something that blew in from far away, something that has nothing to do with you. This storm is you. Something inside of you."

- Haruki Murakami

After attending the Celebrate Recovery large group for over a year, I decided to join the step study they offered. The twelve steps they teach through this class are based on biblical principles, using Jesus' Sermon on the Mount and the beatitudes to deepen our understanding of the process. Each step is tied to a scripture, so we can see how God is there to support us as we work through them. CR is meant to help with any kind of hurt, habit, or hang-up, not only addictions to substances.

The women in the room ranged from addict to co-dependent, survivor of abuse to overeater. We would sit around a set of tables each week and review the homework we completed for the lesson. Each lesson was tied into one of the twelve steps.

I remember sharing my five-minute introduction testimony for the first time, sitting in a circle of about twenty-five strangers. I kept my eyes focused on my paper as I read a few short pages about my life. I was surprised to find so many women with tears in their eyes when I looked up. This showed me for the first time that my story elicited emotion from those that had never experienced anything similar in their own lives.

It caught me off guard. I had expected to find judgment on the faces of the other women, or even pity. Not sadness. Seeing their response made me wonder why I still wasn't able to feel any of the emotions everyone else seemed to be feeling.

The step study class was forty weeks long. Each week, we peeled back another layer of the proverbial onion and learned so much about each other and ourselves. I connected with a woman who was the mother of an addict, and through the whole class, her son was out on the streets using. We learned to see through the other person's eyes and shared advice on how to handle certain scenarios. My own mother still hadn't come to fully trust that I was staying clean. This woman's son would often try to manipulate her while he was high. It was interesting to have so many different issues and perspectives in one room, but somehow it worked.

I also really connected with the leader of the group, Jullie, a woman who had completely turned her life around and poured love into all of us that sat around her table. She would eventually become one of my greatest mentors—someone I turned to for advice and support. She stepped into the role of a second mother, a trusted confidant, and a loyal friend as the years continued.

The fourth step took me through a journey of looking more deeply at the things I had done while in my addiction. The longer I stayed clean, the more detached and different I felt from the person I was when I'd done them. But I still had a deep-rooted guilt in the pit of my stomach. Some days, that guilt wouldn't allow me to even face myself in the mirror.

I had been so many things in active addiction: a thief, a bully, an adulteress, a liar, a deadbeat mother, a bum. Those words felt like they'd been scrawled across my face in bold, black ink, so that everyone who looked at me could tell exactly who I was underneath the mask of a girl at the shelter who was just trying to piece her life back together. It would take many more fourth steps and several different therapists before I came to fully trust that I had processed through all the years of depravity that I'd lived through, and it started right there in that class.

The ninth step taught me how to apologize for the pain I'd caused over the years. I had to work up the boldness to stand in front of the person I had harmed and own up to my mistakes. I sat down at a restaurant with my little sister, Stevie, to make amends to her in person. I poured out the written list of all the things I'd done to hurt her over the years. I truly was sorry for all that I had done to steal her adolescence, expose her to so much violence, and miss pivotal moments in her life while I was too lost in survival mode to be there for her. By the end of the conversation, our relationship felt genuinely restored. We ended it with a tear-stained hug and a promise to always be there for each other.

I wrote and mailed my mother a letter. She had never been one for huge displays of emotion. I knew a letter that she could read on her own would be more meaningful to her. She called me after she read it and said for the first time, she really felt like I meant what I said, and that maybe I had actually made it out, for real this time. My mother had remained present in my life throughout my entire addiction, and while she has struggles of her own, and there have been many fights and disagreements over the years, she never fully abandoned me. I have always been grateful for that.

My older sister, Breana, accepted my amends with grace and said that my recovery was teaching her about those last days that she'd spent with our dad during his active addiction, right before he died. Something that had been so hard to understand was silently revealed to her. She started to see, through talking to me, that a person on drugs is not the same person when they are clean. The influence of narcotics changes the way we think, the way we move and speak, and the way we live. Most importantly, it negatively affects the way that we interact with those that we love most, especially family. Narcotics steal our ability to understand how to be aware of the fears, thoughts, and feelings of others.

Making amends to Carter was a little different because he was only ten years old, but I still chose to do it. His simple response was so pure. He calmly said, "It's okay, Mom. You were sick. It wasn't your fault."

He somehow understood so much more than I thought he would at such a young age and he never blamed me for anything. He walked in graceful acceptance and was kinder to me than I deserved. I know this was in part due to how my mother spoke about the reasons why I hadn't been there. But it was also a reflection of who Carter is as a person. His heart is gentle and loving, and that has been evident since he was a little boy.

In addition to seeking forgiveness from others, I also had to work on forgiving both myself and those who had harmed me. I learned that forgiveness is an inside job, and sometimes a lengthy process. It takes personal reflection and a desire to release the bitterness or resentment that has been built up in our hearts for sometimes years. I took the route of letter-writing when it came to this, pouring my heart out onto paper that no one else would ever read to find an acceptance and then release of the harm done to me, as well as taking responsibility for the harm I'd done to myself. I began to feel real peace when I stopped holding blame over the heads of others who probably didn't even think about me at all anymore.

At the end of the nine-month class, we all stood on the stage and shared our experience for a few minutes, followed by a celebration for the graduates. The step study class left me with a deeper understanding of myself than I'd ever had before. I discovered things that I never would have known.

We'd barely even finished the celebration when one of the leaders came up to me and mentioned that the Ministry Leads thought I would make a good leader and wanted to know if I might be interested in becoming a volunteer. The idea that anyone could hear my story and decide I should help lead other people in ministry surprised me. It reminded me of the way I'd felt when I saw Marcus studying to be a pastor in that sober living kitchen so long ago. I agreed to think about it, and then eventually said yes.

Joining the CR leadership team was one of the greatest decisions I've ever made. The title meant I belonged to a group of passionate people who were all there to help guide and support others as they entered into their own recovery journeys. It instantly created a community for me that was like nothing I had ever been a part of before. The ministry leader, Moi, seemed to see something in me that I wasn't able to see in myself. He brought me into the fold and increased my responsibilities within the ministry.

Pastor Moi had endured and healed from childhood wounds that led him to accept the invitation to run the CR at SeaCoast Grace Church. His compassion for people in the middle of turmoil was clear, and he always led with love and grace. Watching him taught me how to be more gentle with people and how to soften my street-born tendency toward confrontation and bluntness. He helped me learn to tap into my natural leadership qualities, to be a part of a team, and to trust someone in authority. His guidance in those early years was monumentally important to the shifts that were happening in my life.

Moi and his wife Lori-Lynn all but adopted me into their family as I continued to live at such a far distance from my own. They welcomed me without judgment and cheered for me through every new obstacle and achievement.

Our team bonded over writing weekly plans for lessons and groups, planning sober holiday events, and supporting each other as we did our best to lead a flock of hurting people to hopeful restoration. The rest of the leaders became like family as well, as I often spent more time with them than with anyone else in my life. I didn't know it at the time, but some of the most authentic relationships I've ever been a part of were developed in those meetings.

I remember the moment that Moi handed me my own set of keys to the church so I could access the building for the groups I was leading. The level of trust that he had in me built me up in ways that I doubt he ever realized. He gave me the opportunity to prove to myself that I was actually becoming a trustworthy person.

Because of his encouragement and support, the rest of the church leadership trusted me as well. They eventually asked me to run the money team at some of their events throughout the year. I would often be walking across the campus with a backpack full of cash donations, reflecting on how the old me never would have made it through even one of these events without running off with all that loot.

I was a part of that Celebrate Recovery ministry for ten years, a leader for eight of them. I have sponsored more than forty women, led four year-long step studies, created skits, wrote lessons and teachings, and helped edit the writings of each person who gave their testimony at our Friday-night meetings of more than 150 attendees each week.

Things went so well for so long. But there was still so much buried inside me. I still struggled to identify how I was feeling on any given day, if I was able to really feel anything at all. The decision to not feel pain anymore followed me well into my recovery. While in my brain,

I was able to think empathetically, my heart and soul could rarely pinpoint what anything actually *felt* like.

With a desire to sort this out, I joined an intensive outpatient therapy through a program called New Life Spirit Recovery. It was a twelve-week program that used writing therapy to help guide the client through various experiences that may have occurred during a season of trauma or isolation.

My counselor was a young lady with stark black hair and tattoos that covered her arms. She was an artist at heart with a subtle prophetic insight. She had a history of her own that allowed her to understand me more deeply and give me gentle suggestions while we worked through some of the more tragic areas of my life. While I had talked about much of it in my fourth steps, there were still many secrets that felt too dark and too ugly to divulge. I chose to dig more deeply into these things privately with her. I knew there were many details that I was holding back on purpose, but there were also many scars that came from a life lived on the streets that had been hidden, even from me.

There are traumas that come naturally with a lifestyle like mine—wounds I've had to revisit and work through. Unwanted sexual encounters left me on edge and avoidant of romantic relationships. Acts of violence I witnessed or took part in lived deep in my subconscious. Being chased, tased, or beaten by men, some angry that I'd bested their girlfriends in a fight, others just wanting me gone after I'd overstayed my welcome, made me tense up anytime a man stepped behind me. The lies I told, the people I hurt, the times I was stalked or locked in unfamiliar rooms all convinced me that very few people were truly safe. The guilt of giving away pieces of myself just to have a place to sleep or shower still lingered somewhere deep inside me. The shame of not raising my son made me question even my part-time parenting abilities. Even the simpler things like squatting in houses without running water left me with triggers and nightmares about overflowing toilets. For years, I kept a blanket and pillow in the trunk of my car, just in case I couldn't go home.

While on the surface, I kept a clear head and a heart of service, on the inside, these things still lived and breathed, just waiting to come up and wreak havoc on my new life.

In the middle of processing these traumas with my new counselor, my good friend and CR brother, Adam, was involved in a motorcycle accident and was placed on life support. This was the first time that my new faith was truly tested. So many of us surrounded him and covered him in prayer. I believed with all my heart that he was going to wake up—that God was going to heal him. So when the time came for his family to make the heart-wrenching decision to take him off the machines that were keeping him alive, I experienced real doubt in God for the first time since I had come to believe.

The day he died, I broke down in uncontrollable sobs. I couldn't even remember the last time I had cried so hard, and the tears flowed for days and days. I was heartbroken over the loss of my friend, but the response to his death felt weird to me.

I was no stranger to losing people I cared about. I had lost countless friends to their addiction or to the dangerous lifestyle that comes with it. I had lost my father, my son's father, and my baby girl, and I had never released emotion in the way I did during this time. I sat in our session one day and poured it all out to my counselor, telling her that maybe God wasn't real after all, and I was hallucinating when I lost my baby and heard a voice. Maybe that voice was just my own thoughts.

No sooner had those words left my mouth than a gentle tapping began at the window. We were several stories up, so the sound caught us both off guard. We turned to look and saw a small bird perched at the edge of the glass, slowly tap-tap-tapping as it stared in at us. We were surprised to see it there, especially since there was no actual ledge for the bird to be standing on.

"I think God sent that little bird for you, Kelsey. Maybe to show you that He hears you and is here for you. We don't always understand why God does what He does, but we do get to practice trusting that He always knows best," she said.

She helped guide me to the realization that my emotional reaction to Adam's death may have created a shift in my ability to feel. That somehow I was experiencing the release of all the grief I had been holding inside for so many years all at once. God was allowing the loss of my friend to break through the hard shell that covered me and restore the emotions that had been buried so deeply. I thought about my childhood, when I felt everything so intensely that I had to find a way to shut it off. The drugs I used did exactly that. It was a revelation—one that revealed more about the inner workings of my mind than I'd ever understood before.

What began as a twelve-week journey stretched into more than eleven months of deep inner healing work before we felt we had truly covered everything. We revisited moments that should have stirred strong emotions when they happened, working to reconnect me with the ability to feel them. I can't say my frozen emotions were completely healed. Even years later, I still struggle to fully identify what I'm experiencing inside. But the journey brought me to a deeper understanding of who I am, and I was finally able to lay down years of guilt and emotional baggage I'd carried for far too long. In that, I began to feel peace.

REFLECT

Working through the twelve steps of CR provided valuable insight for me in the early years of my recovery. It taught me about the root cause of my behaviors and desire to numb out. I believe that this program would be beneficial for anyone. We all have a hurt, a habit, or a hangup that is holding us back from our true potential. Having an organized curriculum to work from and like-minded people walking through the same steps beside you helps build a foundation for the new life we are often seeking when we step into programs like this.

The friendships that the program provided and the support I received from my church was crucial to being able to break free from this idea that I was too different and too dirty to ever be truly welcome in the real world. They helped to restore so much that was broken or missing within me after the kinds of people I'd surrounded myself with and the decisions I'd made throughout my life. For years, I had seen relationships as only transactional—a trade-off of wants or needs. But these people didn't want anything back from me. They were just good people.

Once I had a healthy group of friends, I began to learn that friendship is based on so much more than what we can do for each other. I started to understand the idea that the opposite of addiction is not sobriety—it's connection. I could recognize how so many of my behaviors stemmed from a deep-rooted feeling of loneliness, and as that feeling disappeared, more of my true self came to the surface.

If you are new to recovery, I strongly encourage you to find a group of similar people to go through your new life beside. Remember that all churches, recovery groups, and small groups are not created equal. I recommend visiting a few before choosing where to plant yourself. Ask God for discernment when it comes to selecting where you should be.

If you are a lifelong church-goer, remember that many times, the church needs to reach out to those who are struggling or actively holding on for dear life as they try to change their circumstances. If you have a heart for the lost or the broken, I challenge you to step out of those four walls and look for ways to connect with someone who may be sitting on the side of the road just waiting to have the love of Jesus shared with them, and they don't even know it. So many addicts will never choose to visit a church on their own because they have no idea what they're missing, or they don't even realize that they're welcome.

Learning to navigate through my resurfacing emotions with a safe person is what kept me clean long-term. God only shows us a little at a time when we revisit our dark history. He knows that our simple human minds can't always digest everything from the past all at once, and so He is gracious enough to only reveal pieces along the way. But when those memories do come flooding back, we need to have a plan in place for who we will process them with. A therapist or counselor, a sponsor or mentor, or a trusted confidant or friend is vital to being able to truly dig into and heal from the past.

If you love an addict on a healing journey, I encourage you to be gentle with them. While many of us wear tough exteriors that present as if we are unbothered by it all, and while some may truly feel that way many are hiding layers of painful secrets deep inside. Outbursts of emotion, whether anger or sadness, guilt or shame, are common when processing through our past actions and often, being able to identify which emotion is winning is the most difficult part. The traumas that come with a life of addiction can be unsettling and demoralizing. Digging through those feelings and memories can result in a lot of unwanted actions and behaviors. Be patient, change is coming.

Feeling again helped me understand how my family had loved me all along, but they didn't want my chaos in their lives. Once I got clean and made amends with them, we found a new sense of peace within our relationships. But there may be some relationships that we have to release because they aren't good for us to hold on to. When we let people back into our circle after we've moved on to a different way of life, we risk having some of those old behaviors start to creep back into our daily routines. We need to always keep our distance from anyone not living a healthy lifestyle while in early recovery, no matter how much we love them and want them around. Unfortunately, oftentimes the people who put us at the highest risk of relapse are members of our own family.

REFLECTIVE QUESTIONS

1. Trusting yourself should feel natural, but if you've let yourself down in the past, rebuilding that trust can take time. How much do you trust yourself right now? What new responsibility could you take on to strengthen that trust?

   _____

   _____

   _____

   _____

2. Is there someone in your life you feel you owe amends to? Have you thought about how you might go about making that amends?

   _____

   _____

   _____

   _____

3. When life doesn't go as we hoped or expected, it's easy to start questioning God's will. Can you describe a time when you doubted God? Has your perspective on Him changed since then?

_____

_____

_____

_____

Chapter 18

Conquering Fears

"Stay afraid, but do it anyway. What's important is the action. You don't have to wait to be confident."

~ Carrie Fisher

For the first few years of my recovery, I rarely talked about the time I had spent on Skid Row outside the confines of Precious Life Shelter or the safety of counseling. I somehow believed that associating myself with that place would paint a more realistic picture of just how dirty I had let my life become before finally hitting rock bottom. I allowed myself to only shed light on the areas that I chose. But as I began writing my testimony for Celebrate Recovery, I realized it would be pretty difficult to share my story without including that part of it.

As my testimony was shared more often and in more places, a small group of people started asking if I would join them in serving on the streets of Skid Row. At first, I gave an adamant *no*. My time there was blurred in my own mind, blockaded into a corner in the far reaches of my memory so that I could forget how low I'd gotten and focus more on the here and now. While that time was not all bad, and in the end it is where I actually got clean, I still associated it with a shameful experience—one that I wasn't willing to describe or explore outside of my safety net.

One night, after teaching at CR, a man came up to me. He wanted to talk about my time spent on Skid Row and invited me to attend one of the events that he hosted there. This man had been a police officer. While at one time I would have shied away from talking to him at all, once we started to chat, it really felt like we had many shared experiences, although from opposite perspectives. We shared a common ground in many areas that I never realized existed for most men with a badge. I had rarely spoken to someone at such length who related to my life but wasn't also fighting to stay clean. Someone who could see the stronghold that addiction had on so many people and wanted to find a way to help them, even though he hadn't had to fight that stronghold himself.

By the end of our conversation I had agreed to join him at an event at the Union Rescue Mission as an observer. It just so happened that this event was scheduled on April 7th, which was the six-year anniversary of the day I decided to get clean.

When we pulled into the underground parking garage, I could see the shelter I'd spent those six months living in across the street. All the memories of my time there came flooding back. We set up tables and chairs in the chapel of the shelter, a young pastor gave a teaching, and then my sweet friend Jessica stood on the stage and sang "Amazing Grace." As I listened to her beautiful voice ringing out such powerful words in the small chapel, tears started to stream down my face. They ran under my chin and dropped onto the Bibles and books we had set out for the unhoused. And in that moment, I knew I was supposed to be there.

I joined the volunteer team that same week. Immediately after saying yes, I was terrified of going back. I had a very specific picture in my mind of what we would encounter on those streets. My memories of the time I spent there were of death, violence, rape, hopelessness, and despair. I had somehow forgotten that the men and women on those streets were actual people, and while I had an isolated, bumpy six-month experience, this was their constant reality. That fear was with me for the first few events, as I stayed close to the other volunteers and kept my back against the wall. Slowly, my perspective began to shift, and I became more connected with the people who served with me and the people we served.

Project 54 Outreach was a non-profit organization whose mission was to bring fellowship to the streets of Skid Row. Once a month, we all piled into vans and drove to downtown LA to set up tables, chairs, and pop-up shades. We invited the homeless community to join us for a hot meal and a quality conversation. What set P54 apart from many other services is that we didn't just hand out food and drive away, we sat with people, prayed with them, and built friendships with them. Something as small as remembering someone's name and smiling when they showed up brought so much joy and life back to those streets.

As I reflected on how much I would have loved to attend an event like that during my time living in the shelter, I started to see the people of Skid Row differently. They were human beings, lost and alone, often mentally sick or underdeveloped, isolated and lonely. They were just looking for someone to *see* them.

Eventually, I took on the role of Outreach Lead. Every month, I would take a group of volunteers out to walk the nearby streets and invite the homeless residents back to the warehouse for brunch and fellowship. My unique history allowed me to keep those volunteers who had never ventured into such a place more alert to their surroundings, and I was able to identify when a situation was unsafe or if an area needed to be avoided. Although my heart continued to soften to the inhabitants of these streets, they were still dangerous streets, operating within a set of rules that outsiders didn't know or understand.

We met so many people out there. People like Mike, a homeless veteran who sold individual cigarettes out of his tent on the side of the road. His teeth were blackened from all the years of smoking, and his voice was gruff. He had a rare talent that he'd acquired during his military years where he could look at someone and tell them their ethnicity and ancestry, and he'd use that talent to impress a new volunteer every month. I never saw him get it wrong. He never came to an event, but he always climbed out of his tent with excitement whenever we'd come by.

Pastor Blue was unhoused, but he had carved out a little haven along a side street. He kept the area clean and welcomed anyone who wanted to sit and rest. In the shade, he set out chairs and tubs of water so visitors could wash their hands and feet. A small table, often stocked with donated snacks, stood ready for anyone in need. At every event, we made it a point to stop and greet him. He usually spent more time praying for us than we did for him.

A man named New York was the heart of our ministry, though, as the whole thing had come to exist at his suggestion. His skin was naturally dark but sun-beaten from the two decades that he'd spent on the streets. His addiction was palpable and ran inside his veins just as deeply as his own blood. He protected us from the occasional vultures that would come to our events and start trouble, and we loved him like family, treated him like a brother, and brought him any necessities that he requested. We even got him to leave the streets with us and go into a transitional living home.

He would join us at the church on Sundays and at CR on Friday nights. While I think most people did their best to treat him like one of the crew, he would share with me that he sometimes felt like he was being propped up like some kind of trophy by a few people here and there. I had felt like that myself a few times over the years.

New York could never get used to the changes. Before too long, he sabotaged himself into losing his job and place to stay. He disappeared for a while, and we all searched for him. We weren't surprised to find that he'd ended up right back on the streets, in the exact same spot he'd left from. Not too long after that, he was found dead in his tent. We all grieved for him like grieving for a lost brother, because in the end, that's what he had become to us.

Not long after I left Skid Row myself, my friend, Vee, had been accepted into a program that provided low income housing in downtown Los Angeles. We eventually found each other on social media, and she learned about P54 from my posts.

I remember the day that she came walking up to one of our events. The emotion hit us both as we hugged, and we just stood in that warehouse parking lot and cried. Throughout my time living on Skid Row, Vee had been my true north. She was honest and supportive, and she guided me toward God, even though at the time I didn't really realize that was what she was doing. After years of separation, I was so happy to reunite with my long-lost friend.

As I stood outside of the event space one day, a man came up to me with a fancy camera and asked if he could take some pictures inside the fences.

"I have a photography page on Instagram where I document some of the stories of the homeless. I'd love to get a few shots of what you're doing out here," he said.

We opened up our phones and started scrolling through his page. His photos were powerful. Under each one, there was a short interview in the caption about what the person in the photo was experiencing on the streets.

Suddenly, my jaw dropped. The face in one of the photos belonged to Brandon, the young man who had taken me to rehab more than six years before.

The interview in the caption told the story of how he'd been on the streets for over a year. It said that he now spent time volunteering at the food coalition, helping to feed the homeless. His mom was still living in a van in Santa Monica.

"Hey—do you remember where you saw this guy?" I asked the photographer, pointing at the image of Brandon on my phone.

"Yeah, he was out at the food coalition in West Hollywood. But I couldn't tell you where he went after that. None of these guys stay in the same spot for very long."

I sat with the internal battle of whether or not to drive to West Hollywood and look for pockets of people living on the streets or visit the food coalition to search for Brandon. But I wasn't even sure what I'd be able to do for him if I had found him, so I never went. I still wonder if I should have.

When Brandon's face appeared on the screen, I finally understood the weight of what he had done for me that day. I'd waved him off, but he refused to leave, instead listening to the quiet voice telling him to stay. That choice to idle in the parking lot, welcome me into his car, and then drive around with me, may have changed my entire life. Only God could have lifted me up from that warm concrete and set me on this new path, but He had to work through someone willing. Brandon became the hands and feet of that divine intervention, speaking to me when the rest of the world stayed silent.

I spent five years serving on the streets of Skid Row. The number of volunteers grew, and the items we brought expanded to books, reading glasses, socks, and hygiene products. The people on our leadership team had very little in common other than our desire to serve the community there, but we became like family as well. We all had a true heart for the people we'd met and connected with.

My whole perspective shifted during my years volunteering there, and I found a new understanding and awareness of poverty. As it turned out, my story about the short time I spent living on Skid Row was one that inspired some of the people there to try for more in life than they felt worthy of having. I'd like to believe that I was able to plant a small seed of hope in an often hopeless place—the hope that we can change our circumstances when we're in the midst of desperation.

It was during this time that the holiday store I'd been working at shut down. I got hired at a new job which paid a little more money, with a good boss and the possibility of moving up within the company. I was finally ready to move out of Precious Life Shelter. After five years in my apartment, I had learned as much as they were able to teach me. I'd paid off mountains of debt and found purpose within my roles as leader at Celebrate Recovery and Project 54 Outreach. I was ready to face the world without their protection.

The time I spent there was invaluable, and the kindness I was shown while I was still such a mess speaks to the core values the shelter holds. I was blessed to be loved and nurtured by them for so long, but I can't deny that part of me stayed for as long as I did because I was afraid to leave. Without the parameters set by the program, there was no guarantee that I'd be able to live entirely on my own and not ruin everything I'd been working towards. For years, I kept a mental backup plan for what I would do in certain scenarios, just in case it all came crashing down one day, so stepping out into the world felt scary. But I knew it was time.

My friend, Kirsten, and I started apartment hunting, with a plan to room together. On a whim, I reached out to Irene, to see if there were any vacancies on the property she owned. To our surprise, there were! The day we signed the lease and she handed us our keys felt like the first day of my real adult life, even though I was thirty-three years old. There was still so much I didn't know about adulting and so many what-ifs that made me nervous, but we moved into our new place with excitement and happiness.

Six months later, one of those what-ifs came to fruition when Kirsten lost her job and couldn't afford her half of the rent. She packed up and moved out, and I was on my own, with no idea where the next month's rent money was going to come from. I managed to pay the first $1,400 on my own, but the following month, I wasn't sure where I would get the whole amount again. I didn't mention the situation to anyone, determined to figure it out on my own. There was no way I was going to lose my place so soon after moving in, so I asked God to help me and started looking for someone else to rent her bedroom.

With the first of the month quickly approaching and no solution yet in sight, a friend of mine from CR asked me to join her for lunch. As we sat at the table, she slid an envelope across to me.

"My husband and I were in prayer, and we felt like the Lord was saying you needed this," she said.

I tucked the envelope into my purse and thanked her, not sure what was inside. Once I was home, I opened it to find exactly $1,400 in cash. She didn't know why I needed that money, but in an act of obedience, she just handed it right over to me. God had come through for me again through the hands and feet of another person. A few weeks later I found a new roommate to take the second bedroom.

My new job, which started out as a data entry position at a privately-owned emergency equipment company, had the potential to become a career in office management, AP/AR, and payroll. My boss believed in me, and as his business grew, he held my hand and allowed me to grow with it. He taught me how to do tasks that I never believed I'd be capable of as a high-school dropout and recovered addict. But he saw more in me than just those labels, and for the past ten years, he has included me in daily business decisions and given me authority over various areas. He's always been supportive of my heart to serve others and allowed my long-distance relationship with my son to take priority.

Carter remained with my mother even after I was clean and living on my own. It just never felt right to rip him from the only life he'd ever known to come live with me at the shelter, surrounded by infants and toddlers. Or to let him struggle with me financially while I continued to learn how to live a productive life in my apartment. Instead, my mother raised him well, and I did my best to always be present for him at all the pivotal moments of his life.

This dynamic between me and my mother was not always easy. There were many disagreements and struggles that came with releasing my child to be raised by someone else. There have been times where I felt like I would have made completely different decisions than she did, times when we flat-out screamed at each other over the direction of his life, and times where it felt impossible to accept that I would never be able to take him home with me for longer than a few weeks at a time. But I still believe it worked out exactly as it was designed. Carter and my mother are both living their own testimonies, and I learned to release any expectations of how they will turn out.

Carter was a theater kid. From his first play at eight years old, all the way to his last play of senior year, I never missed a single one. He would spend school vacations and holidays with me, and we were able to create a good, solid relationship built on truth and love. And while I always hoped, deep down, that one day he might want to come live with me, I never pressured him. I was just grateful to have him in my life in whatever capacity I could get.

REFLECT

None of the experiences in our lives are wasted time. Sometimes it takes years to figure out why we ended up in a certain place or lived through what we did. There are some experiences that we go through where we never figure out the why at all, but I do believe that God never wastes a hurt. Whether we use an experience to grow within ourselves, to help another person walk through something similar, or to write it all down in a book one day, I believe there is always a purpose mixed in somewhere amongst our pain.

Facing the scary pieces of our lives head on is one of the most impactful ways to heal. This doesn't always mean going back to the physical location of that fear like it did in my case. It does mean that burying the details of an experience in the confines of our mind and never bringing it to the light only allows that fear to grow. It may not reveal itself outwardly on a regular basis, but it is still there, nestling in a dark corner, keeping us from being fully illuminated.

Stepping in as the hands and feet of Jesus is a sacred calling, one that rests on everyone who claims to follow Him. We're called to lift the broken, care for the fallen, give to the poor, show up for the incarcerated, and respond when He tells us to act. Each of us has a purpose uniquely designed by God, and we rarely see the full ripple effect of a single act of obedience. When Brandon took that one step toward me, it sparked a healing that now flows through me and into the lives of others. Imagine the impact you could have by doing the same. The courage to speak when the world stays silent lives within each of us, and we may never know who the person we help today might become tomorrow.

Walking into a new chapter of life can be intimidating, and the mental stronghold of feeling so far behind the rest of your peers doesn't always help. We are all on individual journeys in this life. There is no perfect time or age to step into the next phase, we just follow the path laid out before us. Placing faith in God and His power takes away the burden of feeling like we need to figure it all out on our own. He never wanted that for us. Instead we should seek Him, ask Him, or lean on Him and do that *first*, before we allow panic and anxiety to encroach upon us.

Not raising my son was a reality that I had to really dig deep to work through. Feelings of failure, or the belief that I had abandoned him, would often create a guilt so tangible that it felt suffocating some days. But over the years, I came to understand that the choices I made were what I believed to be the best for him. Not for me, not for my mother, but for him. I wanted him to have a good life with his friends, with stability, and with love that came from all angles. And not having additional stressors weighing on my recovery allowed me to fight to stay clean and to build a lasting bond with him, especially in those early years.

I often struggle to find words that encapsulate the gratitude I have for my mother, who gave up so much of her own life to take on the role of single parent to my son. If you have a child being raised by someone else, I would encourage you to think of all the other places your child may have ended up if that person had not stepped in for you. We may not always agree with their actions—we may wish things were different, and many of us may take on that fight to bring our children back into our homes—but I hope we always remain grateful for the people who are putting their lives aside to care for the lives of our children.

If you are a caregiver for someone else's child, thank you. Your sacrifice is seen and acknowledged by me and so many others who couldn't get it right but are grateful that you could.

REFLECTIVE QUESTIONS

1. What place in your life, either physical or in memory, do you feel you need to revisit to find healing? What do you think is holding you back from going there?

_____

_____

_____

_____

2. Praying specifically allows God to respond in ways that clearly reveal His faithfulness. Can you recall a time when you prayed for something in detail and received a clear, specific answer? What was it?

_____

_____

_____

_____

3. As a parent or caregiver, building a strong foundation with our children is essential. How would you describe the relationship you have with your child or children?

_____

_____

_____

_____

Chapter 19
Sitting Still

"Learning to be still,
to really be still and let life happen,
that stillness becomes a radiance."

~ Morgan Freeman

The next few years were spent in a life of serving others. I spent my days working to grow within my company and my evenings and weekends volunteering my time through Celebrate Recovery and Project 54. Eventually, I also led a peer support group at Precious Life Shelter, bringing a sense of camaraderie and understanding to the new residents. I worked at strengthening my bond with Carter despite the distance, reconnecting with family members that I hadn't spoken to in years, and building a life for myself in my small Anaheim apartment.

Just as they did for most people, the lockdowns of 2020 brought an immense amount of change for me, my family, and my friends and coworkers. We spent that first year in a state of the unknown, where all the plans halted, all the services stopped, and time seemed to stand completely still. We learned to embrace the stillness and quiet of a life that seemed to be frozen in time for a while.

A few CR team leaders, including myself, still offered weekly meetings to bring lessons and testimonies to our program members through online portals. But it was never quite the same as being able to meet in person. And even once we returned to in-person services, when the restrictions were lifted and a semblance of normalcy came back, things had changed so much that the changes just kept coming for a long time.

When everything was closed, I found myself spending time at a home church with a family that I'd met through a mutual friend. We would spend our gatherings in deeper prayer than I'd ever experienced within the church walls. They brought another understanding of worship to me as we prayed for very specific things and then saw those things come to fruition in unique ways. They prayed for strongholds to be broken and old wounds to be healed. I experienced a level of deliverance and freedom that I never knew existed.

For almost twenty-five years, I had a severe nicotine addiction. So many times throughout my life, I had attempted to quit smoking and failed. I could last maybe five or six days, but before I knew it, I would be back on the patio with a cigarette in my hand. It felt completely out of my control, until one day my friends prayed to break that addiction and deliver me from smoking.

Of course, I went home after and tested if the prayer had actually worked or not. I took one drag off a cigarette, and an image came into my mind. I saw Jesus handing me a gift with both hands. Then I saw myself take that gift and spit in his face. I put the cigarette out and threw away every nicotine item in my house. I quit cold turkey, like I'd tried to do at least thirty times before. This time, there was no withdrawal, no ugly cough, and no stress or anxious thoughts. Just like my addiction to drugs, it was suddenly gone.

My faith deepened as I witnessed miracles and healings, and I began to have more vivid dreams and stronger communication with God. He became so much more than a figure I imagined in the sky. He became my father and my friend. With my commitment to Him increasing and the world starting to slowly open back up, I knew I was walking toward something new.

In one of the most major changes, Pastor Moi was invited to lead a new church. I made the decision to leave SeaCoast Grace and join him at Sandals Church, at the Anaheim campus. I took on new responsibilities there, leading one of their discipleship classes and joining the offering team. Life slowed down a bit again, and we enjoyed the quiet progression from busyness, to nothingness during the lockdowns, to a subtle balance of both. But I had a feeling that an even bigger change was on the horizon for me.

During this time, another devastating loss struck close to home. It just doesn't feel right to tell my story without also telling hers.

I met Ashley in 2005, when we visited the same drug dealer's house at the same time. We hit it off instantly. All the years I spent on the streets, she spent with me. We couldn't have been more different, but our friendship withstood many challenges. We alternated jail stays, defended each other's character, and had each other's backs through the most extravagant situations. If I had a place to stay, so did she. If she was eating, I ate too. Even when everything around us was falling apart, we still laughed when we were together. We couldn't help it.

Ashley got pregnant, moved in with her mom, and got clean and healthy for the baby about a year before my final arrest and eventual recovery. She pulled her life together right there in the same town where we had been homeless and used drugs, even though I couldn't. Not without leaving.

We always kept in touch, even with the distance. I used to go by her house when I'd visit my son, and we'd take our boys out to the park to play while we caught up with each other's lives. We remained friends through drug use, through recovery, through relapse, and through all the highs and lows we each experienced, no matter what.

After a few years, she started dating someone who would eventually bring drugs into her house. She ended up having a second child with him, attaching them to one another for life. So, whenever I'd go visit her, he and his friends would be out in the garage smoking dope. Some of his friends were guys I used to get high with, so they'd come out to say hello and almost always offer to share whatever they were using. They knew that I'd been clean for a while and was living an entirely different life than when they knew me, but they didn't care.

After a couple of visits like this, I told Ashley that I couldn't go to her house anymore. That it was too risky for me to keep showing up and avoiding these offers to get high. We were both heartbroken about it, but she understood that I needed to protect myself, and we maintained our friendship through phone calls and texts. But with the dope around her all the time again, she eventually relapsed. Her life and the lives of her children slowly spiraled out of control.

I tried to get her out of the situation she was in, offering to move them out to where I was, but she always refused. Instead, after he'd been arrested and she'd run out of options, she moved to her grandmother's house in Ohio and cleaned herself up again. Until the day he followed her there and they both relapsed, one last time.

It didn't take long before he was arrested in Ohio. Without him, she ventured out to buy dope on her own. And one day, the bag of dope she bought was cut or mixed with something nasty—probably fentanyl. She ended up dead on her bedroom floor, leaving behind a nine-year-old son and three-year-old daughter.

The sadness that came from losing my best friend to an overdose after so many years clean is a weight that has stayed with me, constantly resting in my deepest thoughts. Despite witnessing countless deaths over the years, it was her passing that made me question my own survival. I couldn't help but wonder how I could be saved while she was not. Why was I spared from addiction while she lost her life? Where was the same grace for her mistakes that I'd been granted time and again? What separated me from her same fate, that I made it out for good and she didn't? Some might call this survivor's guilt, and maybe that's part of it, but to me, it's more about coming to terms with the fact that I may never fully understand the "why." I may never know how God chooses whom He saves.

The sad reality is that addiction does not discriminate, and it takes lives every single day. No one is immune to the possibility of buying a bad batch, taking a little too much, or having their body shut down after too many hits.

As I dug deeper into a life of prayer during my grief, I could no longer deny that God was calling me to move out of California. I wasn't sure where I was meant to go, or why, but the feeling took root in me and wouldn't go away. In an attempt to figure out the answer, I prayed a very specific prayer and asked for a very specific sign.

Since God had used birds to guide me in the past, I asked for a bird. I decided to choose between three states where some of my friends had relocated and where I might live too: Montana, Missouri, and Idaho. I asked God to send me a red bird for Montana, a bluebird for Missouri, and a yellow bird for Idaho. I don't think I'd ever even seen a yellow bird before until a few weeks after I prayed that prayer.

Suddenly, I began to see yellow birds—goldfinches—all over the place, in groups of three or four, flying through the sky, perched on fences, or flying past windows. I couldn't have denied their presence if I wanted to, and I understood that this was the clarity I needed to go where I was being called. So, I bought a ticket to fly out to Idaho and visit my friends, Meg and Vienna, who had moved there recently. I planned to watch for an open door—a final piece of evidence to show me that I belonged there.

In Idaho, I told Vienna this story—about asking for a specific sign, and about how clearly I had received it. She looked at me thoughtfully for a moment.

"Did you know my family is Native American?" she asked.

"No, I didn't know that," I said.

"When I was born, I got a Native American name."

I felt a rush of excitement before I asked her. "What was it?"

"Yellow Bird." She smiled.

Later, I sat in a restaurant with Meg while she offered me a place to stay with her family on her property. Her new tattoo caught my eye. It was small yellow birds, freshly inked on her chest.

Three months later, I gave away almost everything I owned, packed up my car, and drove to Boise. I moved into Meg's studio-sized back house and waited patiently to see where life was headed.

While I waited, I finally made progress toward something I'd been working toward for over ten years: getting my criminal record expunged. For me, expungement meant a lawyer needed to go back to court to show that I'd turned my life around. If the judge agreed, the charges would be erased and the rights I'd lost would be restored. After all this time, I had the chance to finally wipe that invisible "F for felon" off my face.

It had taken me more than a decade to pay off the entirety of my court fees and fines, which totaled more than twelve thousand dollars. That was the first requirement. I called the public defender's office in the county where I'd served my time, and they walked me through the rest of the process. We started with the felonies, since those were the toughest to clear. I had to show proof of any programs I'd finished, any ways I'd served my community, and at least five personal letters from people willing to vouch for me.

I put out a request for letters to my fellow volunteers, pastors, sponsees, and friends. Three months later, my court date was approved. More than twenty people wrote letters for the judge expressing their support of my venture, sharing stories of the growth they'd witnessed in me, and asking the court to grant me the opportunity to start over. I was nervous as I sent the letters off to the attorney and waited patiently to hear back from the judge.

Scheduling the court date took longer than expected as they waited for reports from probation and verified some of the programs I'd completed. But eventually, my expungement was granted. I was no longer a felon, after wearing that "F" for more than eighteen years.

The next steps taken, which were to remove the misdemeanors, went a little more smoothly, but I had so many of those that we needed multiple court dates with the judge. Within a year, I'd been approved for a full expungement, and every crime I'd ever been convicted of was wiped off my record.

I had done many things over the years to step into the new life I was living, but the stains of my past always lingered in my criminal record, reminding me of the years I spent in selfishness and a total disregard for society. It felt like one of the greatest victories of my recovery to no longer have those convictions holding me back.

Aside from the calls and emails to keep the process moving, my life was quiet—quieter than it had been in years. I was learning how to live simply in a season where so much was still unknown. I didn't know exactly why I was in Idaho, or why I'd been called away from the first eleven years of my recovery and all the places I'd served. But I was here, ready for whatever was next.

Some days, as I sat in the stillness, I wondered if I'd heard God wrong and moving to Idaho had been a mistake. I sought places to serve, and I would get right up to the door when something would always seem to go wrong, and that particular door would shut. I tried to volunteer at troubled youth homes and rescue missions, through churches I visited and people I met, but nothing ever seemed to work out. Confused about my purpose, I continued to sit in the stillness and wait for direction. In that time, I formed some new friendships, read some new books, and explored my new state.

REFLECT

There is a difference between sitting in stillness and sitting in isolation. Learning to sit still and wait takes practice and focus. Listening for God's voice and seeking His direction is an art, a journey, and a gift of exploration.

I think asking for a specific sign to help us along isn't always the right move, but when it comes to big decisions, it was important for me to feel certain. A move to a new state was a major change, and it meant leaving behind so many vital parts of my life—from the people and places I served, to my support system and family. Stepping out in faith was an act of trust and boldness.

Losing people to addiction is never easy, and it gets even harder the longer we've stayed clean ourselves. Sometimes we make choices that put us at greater risk of relapse, like choosing to stay in relationships with active users. We may be strong in our recovery, but if we are surrounding ourselves with the drug we once lived for, it is often only a matter of time before we slip back into those old behaviors. The harsh truth is that drugs are getting increasingly more dangerous, and we are seeing more lives lost from using them than ever before.

I am not someone who believes the phrase "once an addict, always an addict." I believe we can be *fully* healed from our addictions and set free from the stronghold they had on us. But we must tread lightly and step into our new identities with our feet firmly planted in that truth. If we waver, or if we doubt that we have been healed, we risk setbacks.

Expunging a record can be a grueling process, and it comes with a lot of work and preparation. But it is so valuable to the journey. I never imagined I'd experience such a feeling of freedom and accomplishment. Even though daily life didn't change much once that "F" was gone, my confidence grew, and an ugly piece of my past was finally buried. There are people who are willing to help us get that fresh start and new beginning, once we take the first steps that lead us to ask them for help.

REFLECTIVE QUESTIONS

1. Quieting our minds and sitting in stillness takes practice. How difficult is it for you to be still and be present in the quiet?

_____

_____

_____

_____

2. Can you recognize what you believe is your purpose in this life? What do you feel it is, and are you actively living it out?

_____

_____

_____

_____

3. Serving others can help us move beyond our own struggles and use our talents to make a difference. Are there places where you'd like to serve? What's holding you back from doing so?

_____

_____

_____

_____

Chapter 20
Coming Full Circle

"I love when people that have been through hell walk out of the flames carrying buckets of water for those still consumed by the fire."

~ Stephanie Sparkles

As I embraced my Idaho life, I began to settle on the idea that I was in this season of waiting for a reason. It gave me the time that I needed to build relationships with the locals. I made a sweet new friend who had an available one-bedroom apartment above her salon, and after nine months in the cozy studio with Meg and her family, I moved into my own beautiful new place. I made friends with some of the stylists downstairs, joined a Bible study, and leaned into the newness of it all.

One of my friends, Sara, knew that I'd been seeking a place to serve and asked if I might be interested in prison ministry. At first, I was not. Just like with Skid Row, jail was not a place I had ever planned to step into again. It was a time in my history that I didn't give much attention to anymore, allowing myself to be free from that chapter of confinement. I honestly didn't think I would be accepted to volunteer there anyway, after all the other doors I'd tried to walk through had slammed shut. Even still, I agreed to join her at the volunteer training, just to see, and so she wouldn't have to go alone.

Simultaneously, one of the ladies from the salon downstairs handed me a book, *The Girl in Your Wallet* by Teresa Nickell. I opened the book, and from the very first page, I felt connected to this woman—to her story and her passion. I finished it easily and found that her last few chapters talked about serving in a prison ministry. That felt a little too coincidental to not mean something. So when I walked into that prison training, a few days after I'd finished reading the book, I had a different attitude about it.

I wanted to serve there, if that was where God wanted me to serve, and to share a little hope with these women who still needed to figure out what I had learned so many years before: how to stop the cycle of homelessness, addiction, and incarceration. Sara and I sat in that three-hour training wondering what we would even do in the prison, what we would teach, or how we would figure that out.

There was a woman sitting a few rows ahead of us, and the back of her head kept grabbing my attention. I didn't know why, but I felt drawn to this person for some reason, like I recognized her even though I was still relatively new in town and didn't know very many people yet. When the training was over, she stood and turned. It was Teresa Nickell, the author of the book I had just finished reading, attending the same training that I was.

"Hi, are you Teresa Nickell? I just finished reading your book! It was amazing. We actually have quite a bit in common."

"Yes, I am, I'm so glad you enjoyed it! Actually, the prison asked if I might be interested in doing a workshop based on my book and I am in need of teammates. Would you maybe want to get some coffee and have a chat?"

A few days later, Teresa and I sat in a coffee shop at our first meeting. I shared some of my history with her, and we found that we had a lot of similarities in our stories and had overcome many of the same obstacles. We talked for a long time and shared ideas. By the end of the meeting, I had agreed to work with her to build a workshop for the women at South Boise Women's Correctional Center. Eventually, Sara joined us as well.

But it wasn't until our second meeting that she said something that really lit up inside me.

"I don't know why, Kelsey, but I feel like more than a workshop is going to come out of us meeting. I think we are going to find that your book is in here, as well," she said, taking a sip of her warm drink.

"Oh? People have been telling me for years that I should write one. I've always enjoyed writing. I'm just not sure how to start or where to go with it once it's done."

"Well, maybe I can be of some help in that area," she said.

Out of that meeting came two new beginnings: the writing of this book and my first steps inside the prison walls. We got to work creating something incredible to share with the ladies behind the fence, combining our two experiences into lessons and activities. I got started with my fingers on the keyboard, pouring out the testimony that I felt God was telling me to share. As I journeyed through the writing process, Teresa became a sounding board and supporter, mentoring me and answering my questions while I endeavored to get the words onto the paper.

On our first visit to the prison, we joined a sweet couple who bring weekly Sunday church services to the ladies. I walked in feeling uncertain, still not fully convinced that this was where I was being led, even though the pieces had fallen together so easily. Sara, Teresa, and I sat in the back and took it all in as I prayed silently for a sign that this was the place I was meant to be.

Close to the end of church, the ladies started to get a little rowdy. The leader held up her hand and started singing a song to settle them down. Slowly, the residents joined in, singing "Amazing Grace." The words echoed through the small prison classroom, and I felt a deep understanding that God was using the same sign he'd given me in that small Skid Row chapel so many years before.

One year later, and we are teaching inside prisons and re-rentry programs, bringing *The Girl on Fire Life-Skills* workshop to currently incarcerated or recently released women. We share our experiences, take part in group discussions, laugh at light-hearted skits, cry at emotional activities, and build solid relationships with the participants. We pour into these women, and they pour into us. They remind us how miraculous it is that we've not only made it out of a broken cycle, but that we now get to lead others along the same path so they can get out too.

Going back behind those brick walls and wire fences was intimidating at first, but many of the women we found there are desperate for change. They are well aware of their shortcomings and don't need any of us to remind them of what they've done wrong. They are thirsty for love, hope, and support. If we can do nothing else inside those buildings, we can give them that.

The more time I spend with these women, the more I see how desperate we all are for someone to truly see us—not the person we project to strangers, but the person we are fighting to hold onto as we go through this often harsh and cruel world. To be truly seen by another is rare, but can be life-changing.

According to the Bureau of Justice Statistics, Idaho has the largest female incarceration population in the whole country, but is one of the lowest in crime because of their strict drug policies and laws. The number of women in prison here has increased by five thousand percent since 1980. Reading those numbers caused me to question what is happening to the women here, and what we can do to help stop the cycle of imprisonment and be an example of how starting over is possible for them.

The question these numbers really answered, though, is why God sent me to Idaho in the first place, and why every door of service I tried to walk through slammed shut, until I walked through this one. I'm not sure how far this new ministry will go or how much we'll be able to help through it, but I know that oftentimes willingness alone is all God needs to make a difference through someone.

Once I'd been in Idaho for about eighteen months, a conversation began between myself and my son Carter that I'd been waiting for since he was a young boy. Now, a twenty-one year old man, ready to start his journey into adulthood, he sat down with me and said that he'd been considering joining me here in Idaho, if I was open to it. He had already visited me several times, so he understood what my life here was like.

While on the inside, I wanted to leap up with excitement and jump up and down for a while, on the outside I stayed cool and responded with, "Sure, that sounds great. I'd love that." After all the years he'd spent living with his grandma, it was exciting to hear that he wanted to live with me now. So many people never get that second chance.

A few short months later, he was here, and we were hunting for a new home to share together, as a family, just as it was always meant to be. On a whim, we decided to try and look for a house to rent instead of an apartment. After applying to a few, a private owner said yes! I had always believed that a house was too far out of reach for me, but had finally arrived at a place in my life where it wasn't that distant after all.

I moved into my very first house, after years of homelessness, couch surfing, living in shelters, small apartments and back houses. Carter and I stepped into our new home, together. And it has been an exciting journey already.

There have been late-night talks of hopes and aspirations, emotional conversations about my messy past, quirky banter, and our ever-coveted "boogie breaks," where we take just a few minutes during a stressful or dull moment for a quick dance session to bring in a little happiness to our day.

I've watched him accomplish goals that he'd been putting off and shine with pride once they were done. I've seen him step into new responsibility and make life decisions. More than anything, though, there has been a healing and a fresh connection forming between us since he's been here. I am so grateful that I have been given this time with him in this season, before he heads out to face the world on his own.

Over the last fifteen years of recovery, my life has come full circle in every way. I never imagined, after so many years of selfishness and living only for my own wants and needs, that I would now live a life built around serving and supporting others. I have kept my career in that same small business by working remotely for a boss that champions my journey, even all the way to Idaho. I have my only son here with me, and our home is comfortable and peaceful. I have strong, loyal friendships that withstand time and distance. I have found confidence within myself as a published author. I have become a bridge between the addict and the friend or relative that can't understand why they just can't get it together. I have learned how to use my abilities to build workshops and create programs through Celebrate Recovery, non-profit organizations, and now prison ministries, where I stand up and speak to groups of people to encourage them to believe that change is possible, and to show them that I am a living example of that.

I am no one special. Anyone can step into a brand new life with the right mindset and the willingness to fight for something different.

The danger of staying in active addiction is getting more and more serious all the time. I can count on one hand the number of longtime friends from Las Vegas who made it out alive and are not holed up in prison for the rest of their lives. The severity of that truth hits me deeply. I never want to take my survival for granted.

The drugs are laced with fentanyl more than ever before, with even marijuana testing positive for traces. There's not a dealer in the world who truly cares about whether or not they take you out. The life that comes with continued use of these drugs is no life at all.

Addiction is not a hopeless situation, and getting out is not a distant dream, even if it feels completely unattainable some days. Recovery starts with a single step out of the fire. Salvation starts with a single prayer into redemption. God promises to restore everything that the locusts have eaten, and I can tell you that He keeps His promises.

No matter what wrongs we have done or ways that we have messed up, we are not our past mistakes. We do not have to carry the weight of shame on our backs like a backpack full of bricks for the rest of our lives. We get to come to the foot of the cross and hand it over to the one who lived and died for us. We have the privilege of starting over whenever we want and choosing a different life for ourselves.

When we survive something that fought so hard to destroy us, we owe it to the rest of the people fighting that same battle to share how we made it out of the flames and into the beauty of restoration. All the days I spent sitting in a cell, or in a shelter, or on the side of the road—how different could it have been if I'd found even a glimmer of hope in the pages of a book or the words of a testimony? Would I have found a renewed strength within myself to try a little harder if there were more stories that talked about getting to the other side of an addiction, or a hard life, or a tragic loss?

If we've lived to tell the tale, we should tell it.

I have learned that writing my story down was always going to be part of the journey. It's been an exploration of even deeper healing and a time of personal reflection. What happens with this book is not up to me, but my prayer would be that it finds its way into the hands of those that need it the most and that those who read it feel inspired to look at their own journey.

No matter where we started off in life or where we're going, we all have a story. And if you've been answering my questions along the way, you've just taken the first steps toward writing yours down.

I can't wait to read it someday.

REFLECTIVE QUESTIONS

1. Sharing our story as a testimony of change and redemption is so powerful. If you were to write your memoir, what would the first sentence be?

   _____

   _____

   _____

   _____

2. What parts of your own story do you find most inspiring?

   _____

   _____

   _____

   _____

3. What stops you from writing it all down?

   _____

   _____

   _____

   _____

A Final Note
Breaking Down Walls

"Love recognizes no barriers. It jumps hurdles, leaps fences,
penetrates walls to arrive at its destination full of hope."

~ Maya Angelou

Welcome to the end! Or could it be a new beginning? Did you travel all the way to the back of the book with grace and leisure, or did you slide in like a player slides into home base on the baseball field, covered in dirt and gratitude that it's finally over? Either way, I'm glad you made it.

There was a time when I believed that once I got past the next obstacle, everything would be smooth sailing for a while. But if I've learned anything in the last fifteen years of recovery, it's that there will always be a new challenge to overcome, a new hurdle to leap (or throw myself) over, another roadblock that has to be moved out of the way or pushed past. I guess that means that the story never really ends, does it? It shifts and changes, but it still goes on.

So then, how do you close a story that's still being written? One thing I know for certain is that I can't predict the future. I never would have imagined as a child in a dysfunctional home, a teenager running the streets of Las Vegas, an addicted nomad roaming the beaches of SoCal, a homeless twenty-something fighting for her life on Skid Row, a grieving mother, or a fearless leader, that one day I'd move to Idaho, write a book and hang out in prisons willingly. But since I'm here, I think I'll try and make a difference somehow. I'll try and keep the story going.

And to you, dear reader—I hope you'll do the same. I hope you will look deep inside yourself and find your own story. And if you don't like the road that the current journey is taking you down, then change direction. You are the narrator and storyteller of your life. You have the power to knock down the walls and barriers set before you. You have a God who is guiding you and championing for your victory, in whatever way that you understand Him. He is the fourth man in the fire with you, when it feels like everything is ablaze, you are never alone.

While your earthly father may be like mine, allowing you to touch the fire again and again until you learn your lesson, your heavenly father climbs into those flames with you, protecting you from the inferno that wants to burn you up. And even if you don't know it yet, you have people like me who believe in you without even knowing you.

My challenge to you is to keep pressing on, to never give up, and to fight for your own life or the life of someone you love. To never let go of your own hope that things can get better because I promise, they can and they do. Hold firm to the belief that something can change and it will.

I also encourage you to search for your own faith and find peace in a God who loves you. Because only God has the power to burn away all of your pain, fear, and anxiety, as well as the ugliness of your past, so your heart can be opened up for a renewed sense of self-love and self-worth. Perhaps this means finding and joining a church or a small group, volunteering your time for a cause you support, or reaching out to hold the flashlight for the person seeking redemption after you. I believe that welcoming Jesus into your life will help you find the peace that you've been chasing.

Keep going. You're gonna make it.

Kelsey

*"Though your sins are like scarlet, they shall be as white as snow,
Though they are red as crimson, they shall be like wool."*

~ Isaiah 1:18

To see images that help bring Kelsey's story to life, or to learn more about what she's doing inside the prisons and other recovery facilities, visit her website: kelseyjharris.com

or scan the QR code below

kelseyjharris.com

About the Author

KELSEY J. HARRIS is an author from Las Vegas, Nevada. She started experimenting with drugs in her early teenage years which ultimately led to addiction, homelessness, and multiple incarcerations. After finding freedom through her faith in God, she has been clean for fifteen years and has found her life's purpose of helping others impacted by addictions find healing and share their own stories.

In addition to authoring *Touching Fire*, Kelsey has held long-term leadership roles with Celebrate Recovery in Southern California and a Skid Row non-profit organization in Los Angeles. She has spent multiple years guiding both men and women through the process of writing and sharing their own testimonies and facilitating a peer support group at the life-saving pregnancy shelter she once resided in.

Currently living in rural Idaho with her son and a ginger cat, Kelsey is the co-creator and facilitator of *The Girl on Fire Life-Skills Workshop* for current and formerly incarcerated women.

For more information about Kelsey Harris' healing journey and passion for helping others, visit www.kelseyjharris.com.

Acknowledgments

There were many people who played a role in more than just the hours spent on this book, but also to the restoration of my sanity and to my recovery journey. To each of you I extend my deepest appreciation and gratitude.

My sister, Breana, Master of Creative Writing, for your encouragement, support, book collaborations, editing skills, and constant reminders that I am a better writer than I think.

My sister, Stevie, for all the support you have shown me over the years in every aspect of my recovery journey from the very first day I decided to try again, until the day you got a dog.

My son, Carter, for your unconditional love no matter what, and for watching the cat while I worked countless side jobs to pay for this book.

My mother, for raising my son well and never giving up on me. Words aren't enough.

My California bestie, Ryan Gesicki, for the countless hours you spent with me on video chats discussing this book and its various needs, including the need for me to not lose my mind through the process.

My Precious Life Shelter family: Theresa Murphy, Wanda Crawford, Martha Alejandre, Tammy Krause, Wendy Wicker, and Kathy Ruscheinsky, for showing me love and kindness when I had no one else in the world.

My Stats crew: Fred White, George Yocky, Tonya Cervantes, and Patricia Jordan for dealing with me when I was fresh off the streets, young and dumb, but loving me anyway.

My friends, Moi & Lori-Lynn Navarro, the older siblings I got to choose, for your love and support, your creative ideas, and for always having my back and sharing your vast knowledge of contracts.

My sponsors, Irene Haas-Knight and Jullie Giraud, for the years of guidance, listening ears, and shoulders for me to lean and sometimes cry on. Thank you for carrying me through.

My friend, Lucinda Wong, for the phone calls filled with power prayers, victory mindsets, and reminders that no man can stop what God has purposed for his glory. I am so grateful for your friendship.

My adventure buddy, Laura Helbert, for your creative insight on the cover design and your excitement about this book in the moments when I felt scared to death.

My boss, Gil Garcia, and work brother, Jacob Daboul, for sticking it out with me all these years as my heart to serve often outweighed my desire to work–but you still let me keep my job, always supported me, and encouraged me to grow.

My writing mentor and prison workshop partner, Teresa Nickell, for your unwavering support along the way and your pointer finger in the air. This book would not exist without you.

My publishing coach, Patrick Snow, an incredible encourager and cheerleader, for your weekly meetings that were filled with support, enthusiasm and absolutely wild ideas.

All the friends I've made and family I've built, and every single person who ever told me that I should write a book someday, this one's for you. I hope you buy it.